$10—
2

MW01062085

Cougar

Cougar

A GUIDE FOR
OLDER WOMEN DATING
YOUNGER MEN

Valerie Gibson

Illustrations by Graham Pilsworth

KEY PORTER BOOKS

National Library of Canada Cataloguing in Publication Data

Gibson, Valerie
    Cougar : a guide for older women dating younger men

ISBN: 1-55263-410-8

1. Middle aged women. 2. Young men. 3. Dating (Social customs). I. Title.

HQ801.G5185 2001   646.7'7   C2001-901686-7

The publisher gratefully acknowledges the support of the Canada Council for the Arts and the
Ontario Arts Council for its publishing program.

We acknowledge the financial support of the Government of Canada through the Book
Publishing Industry Development Program (BPIDP) for our publishing activities.

Key Porter Books Limited
70 The Esplanade
Toronto, Ontario
Canada M5E 1R2

www.keyporter.com

Design: Peter Maher
Electronic formatting: Heidi Palfrey

Printed and bound in Canada

01 02 03 04 05 6 5 4 3 2 1

For Pepi

Contents

The Cougar Rules

1. Feel sexy, be sexy, dress sexy.

2. Ignore anyone who says you shouldn't.

3. Avoid sex on the first encounter.

4. Well, okay, if you absolutely **must**.

5. Keep control when hunting.

6. Well, up to the third martini anyway.

7. Think short-term, not long-term.

8. Okay, think long-term if the sex is **amazing**.

9. Carry condoms.

10. Use them.

COUGAR (according to Miriam Webster's Collegiate Dictionary): a large powerful tawny brown cat formerly widespread in the Americas but now reduced in number or extinct in many areas.

COUGAR (according to twentieth-century reality): single, confident, female predator who likes to date younger men. Species is currently increasing in number and can be found in urban jungles throughout the world.

PUMA: a younger woman.

PREY: any willing male who is six or more (preferably much more) years younger than a cougar.

Birth of a Cougar

I DIDN'T HIT my stride until I turned forty.

Oh, I'd had four marriages by that time and had led quite the wild life but, somehow, I'd never been able to get it all together. I guess I was the consummate late bloomer. Lucky for me that my "awakening" coincided with Nature's Last Stand—that pivotal moment when a woman's hormones make their final, frantic dash through the body before leaping like lemmings over the menopausal cliff.

So, there I was—forty years old and hotter than a chili pepper. Many might say that I've always been like that (especially my mother, who blamed her stomach ulcers on my wanton ways). But my various forays into loving and marital relationships with men my own age or older always seemed to end in tears. Theirs, I must add. I always sailed on unscathed into yet another disastrous liaison.

Forty found me permanently attached yet again. Four years later I wasn't. During those crucial years, I set out in a new direction. After spending my entire life on men's dreams, I found myself wondering what had happened to my own. Did I mention that I also made an exciting and enjoyable discovery? Younger men.

My then-marriage crumbled beneath a mountain of problems, not the least of which was the close proximity in my daily working life of an extremely handsome and well-built young man. A proximity that became so close we couldn't be pried apart. My marriage split acrimoniously and, at forty-four, I found myself homeless, jobless, and credit card–less, not to mention broke.

Yet along with the new (and at times seemingly insurmountable) challenges of emotional and financial survival, I found that being forty-four, single, and hotter than a chili pepper was by no means the social drawback one might expect—or be led to believe. In fact, far from finding myself alone and dateless, I appeared to be just what quite a number of men—younger men—were after. They certainly turned out to be what I was after.

Far from panicking and running the other way (as was still expected in those restrictive and societally condemning days), I jumped right into the deep end and became an outspoken and visible "cougar"—a single, older woman who prefers to date younger men, and is proud of that choice.

I wasn't worried about what people would think. I didn't even consider hiding my predatory ways. I simply roared out into the world and began to sample the pleasures of relationships with younger men—without guilt.

Imagine my surprise when I discovered that, at that time, most other older women didn't share my newfound confidence. While many were busy doing exactly what I was doing, they were just as busy hiding it. Why? Because society has a double standard, they said. It's okay for older men to date much younger women; in fact, society tends to give its approval to such liaisons. When it comes to older women, however, there are very different rules. Older men who date younger women are looked on with admiration (by other older men) and called virile. Older women who date younger men are scorned (by both sexes) and called foolish. And much worse.

Cougar poop!

Although I may have been a pioneer in the art of the cougar hunt, I'm glad to say that this delightful pastime has since not only become acceptable to most of society (there are still diehard pockets of resistance in the urban jungle), but also taken its proper and necessary place in the world of alternative relationships.

The Cougar Defined

BEING CALLED COUGARS may be a new approach, but older women who love younger men have been around forever. Could history have gone like this?

While the older male cave dwellers were out on the hunt, the older women in the cave were happily stalking their own prey—the younger men left behind.

Later, as ye olde knight cantered off to war, his lady love waved cheerily from the castle wall while a young knave worked frantically to unlock her chastity belt.

In Elizabethan times, many young women trod the well-worn path of marrying older men. For most, especially if royal, the phrase "losing your head" became unpleasantly real. Older women knew better: young men were far less lethal.

Edwardian cougars took the "tasty bait" approach. They lay around pale, alluring, and interesting while young swains fed them passionate poems. Then they pounced.

Times of war were particularly plentiful. While the older men marched off to serve, cougars did their part by devoting their attention to an eager generation of pups only too willing to "serve" in a different capacity.

Despite the sexual revolution in the '60s and '70s, when everything that moved was considered fair game, older women who dated younger men were still taboo. This made cougars growl with frustration. When the female liberation and power-surge days of the '80s and '90s arrived, cougars were released from the societal cage. It didn't take long for them to make full and powerful use of their new freedom.

A Roaring Trend

THE NEW, FREE COUGAR is a unique breed. Although celebrities such as Elizabeth Taylor, Madonna, Mary Tyler Moore, Cher, Glenn Close, Raquel Welch, Joan Collins, Mae West, Goldie Hawn, and Linda Evans may have helped to make cougars publicly acceptable, it's the average older woman who is turning the hunt into a roaring trend.

Today's cougar is full of life, sparkling with joie de vivre, and seemingly ageless (although this may have something to do with major cosmetic surgery). She has a lively, inquiring, and interested mind that's always open to new ideas and thoughts. She keeps up to date with what's happening in the world, and gets along well with younger people—especially younger men.

She is single, older, and often divorced (at least once). She may have come out of a marriage with a hefty share of the spoils and find that she suddenly has more time (and money) to spend on herself and life's special pleasures—such as drinking, carousing, and spending hours making love. She may be a single parent with grown cubs or a nanny, leaving her plenty of free time to hunt.

She's a career women or financially independent. If she is working, her career may have either expanded and soared, becoming so time-consuming that there's not much room for anything else—especially a commitment to a demanding relationship.

She isn't interested in marriage or in having any more children. In fact, she often prefers not to share her den. Sexually hot to trot, she is brimming with confidence and allure—that almost intangible aura that is immediately picked up by the antennae of men who know a fascinating woman when they see one. With a little allure working in her favor, a cougar doesn't have to look like a movie star or a supermodel. She can simply be herself—interesting, active, aware, adaptable, fun, sexy, loving, sensitive, and determined.

Whatever her situation, what the cougar wants at this point in her social and emotional life just happens to match up with what many young men want—hot, satisfying sex with someone who won't be a lifetime or live-in partner. It doesn't hurt if this someone is a pleasure to look at, fun to be with, interesting to talk to, and good for the ego. Someone who can handle more than one martini without falling over is an asset, too.

If she can't get any of that, plenty of steamy sex will do very well.

Cougar Do's and Don'ts

IF BEING A COUGAR is ninety percent attitude, the other ten percent comes down to a cat-like awareness of some basic do's and don'ts. Men in general, and young men in particular, are not attracted to women who fuss, whine, complain, or nag. Cougars don't. They don't discuss aches, pain, illnesses, or surgery. They don't refuse to drive in convertibles. They don't drink and drive (cabs are great for snogging).

What do good cougars do? They have careers and know how to be classy at all times. They know how to flirt, how to hold in their stomachs for hours at a time, and how to handle menopause. They own vibrators, carry condoms, and give fabulous oral sex. They always smell wonderful. They also know the importance of ...

NEVER SAYING ...

- ᵧ Commitment
- ᵧ Retirement
- ᵧ When I was younger
- ᵧ I'm too old
- ᵧ Not tonight
- ᵧ Was it good for you?
- ᵧ When will I see you again?
- ᵧ I love you
- ᵧ Is this too short?
- ᵧ Is this too tight?
- ᵧ Is this too low?

STAYING FIT AND TONED

Cougars know that keeping fit and toned not only helps them look good but also helps stave off all those ailments that end up as the Disease of the Month. Exercise can also increase flexibility and suppleness—two very beneficial assets when it comes to dating sexually adventurous young men. Although they rarely have time to visit a gym—unless they're hunting, that is—cougars never put off exercising. They don't have to. Vigorous sex counts.

MAINTAINING A HEALTHY DIET

While most cougars feel that a diet of martinis and restaurant foods is just fine, they also know that eating nutritiously is an essential part of looking and feeling good. This can be challenging if dating a fast-food addict. Searching out prey who follow a vegetarian diet is one solution; dining alone on "healthy meal" nights is another. Although cougars have been known to skip a meal or two in order to fit into a clingy cocktail dress, obsessive dieting is frowned upon—it's physically damaging and a bore to boot. Smart cougars know that nothing ruins a good date faster than a picky eater.

A word about alcohol. Despite the pleasures and relaxation of it all, moderation (not a cougar word) is the key. Nothing is less attractive than a cougar who's had too much to drink. Mind you, there are times when an evening at home awash with an excess of wine can be both exciting and satisfying. The cardinal rule here? Don't let him stay overnight. Being seen ashen-faced and nursing a hangover in the harsh light of dawn could permanently frighten him off.

DRESSING TO KILL

Cougars are sexy dressers. They wear high heels, short skirts, and great underwear. Most have worked long and hard to be in good shape, and don't see the point in hiding the results of their efforts under loose, baggy clothes. When shopping, cougars will know they've got a hit on their hands if the salesperson wonders if the outfit is too tight, too short, or too young. When it comes to their clothes, cougars don't know the meaning of "age appropriate," unless they're visiting relatives.

Cougars don't own bunny slippers or flannel pajamas (okay, one pair of each, and they come out only on cold, lonely nights). Cougars are not afraid of wearing bright colors, or of standing out in a crowd. (A word about color in the bedroom: Avoid black sheets. They can give a funereal feeling to the proceedings, especially if you're pale.)

Dressing to kill

CARING FOR THEIR COATS

Cougars have modern hairstyles, and they never, ever let themselves go gray. While a number of drugstore products are available, most cougars prefer hair salons, which are always filled with attractive young men who are there specifically to take care of them. Careful cougars also make sure that *all* of their hair—no matter where it might be found—is the same color.

Some cougars prefer their hair short. It's easy to care for and doesn't get tangled during wild sexual encounters. Others like long hair, and ignore anyone who says that it doesn't suit women of a certain age.

Cougars do not let unwanted hair grow anywhere on their bodies. While whiskers look great on a real feline, human cougars should pluck them as fast as they appear. Bristly legs are also a no-no.

EMBRACING AGE-DEFYING TECHNOLOGY

Cougars are not afraid to improve upon nature. They want to look their best, and they're willing to embrace any and all anti-aging techniques. They'll try hormone therapy and photofacials, laser resurfacing and vein removal, Botox and Monobloc. They'll even go under the knife.

Cougars will not, however, share this information with their young man. It diminishes the aura of mystery and indeterminate age that they strive to present. If a two-week recovery period is required, a cougar may have to resort to a little bit of subterfuge. Good excuses include a vacation, a visit to a sick family member, or a trek through the Himalayas. She can then return looking refreshed and rejuvenated—and praising the restorative powers of yak milk.

Why Younger Men?

WHY NOT? For a cougar, they're perfect prey.

Younger men are plentiful and often very willing to be lured. They tend to find cougars irresistible—for their confidence, sleek sophistication, independence, and considerable sexual experience.

Younger men have flat stomachs, firm butts, strong thighs, and ever-ready sexual equipment. They also bring a fresh taste to palates dulled by jaded older men. They are optimistic, enthusiastic, energetic, passionate, and—essential when dealing with the strong and powerful cougar—brimming with youthful stamina.

Younger men never want to leave a party early, and they never criticize your driving. They love your cooking. They love to kiss, walk barefoot on the beach, trek through the woods, sing out loud, dance until the small hours, accompany you shopping (especially for lingerie), and make love in the back seat of the car (yours, usually). Most importantly, they know how to stop your VCR from constantly flashing and can actually program your car radio.

WHAT A COUGAR WON'T GET WITH A YOUNGER MAN

- ⍋ a mid-life crisis
- ⍋ erectile dysfunction
- ⍋ a beer belly
- ⍋ excuses or "headaches"
- ⍋ an ex-wife and kids (okay, maybe one)
- ⍋ Viagra (unless it's for fun and extra stimulation)
- ⍋ objections to condoms
- ⍋ hair dye on the pillow (if there's any, change your stylist)
- ⍋ snoring (if he does you're too exhausted to notice)
- ⍋ use of toothpicks
- ⍋ a two-minute "wham-bam-was-it-good-for-you" sexual yawn every Saturday morning
- ⍋ personal laundry (you send it home with him)

What a Cougar Will Get With a Younger Man

- enthusiastic oral sex
- multiple orgasms
- public affection
- a flat stomach
- a firm butt
- always-ready sexual equipment
- spontaneity
- stamina
- adoration and appreciation
- admiration (from other cougars)
- someone who looks good every morning (no matter what he did the night before)
- did I mention multiple orgasms?

In other words, the older woman/younger man pairing is a most beneficial relationship, and an ideal solution for older women looking for fun. Those licking their wounds—from dating or marrying fading, full-of-baggage middle-aged men—can profit as well. Despite the battle scars, these cougars find that they're still fit, firm, full of life, and hotter than chili peppers. All they want is someone who can say the same.

Cougar Prey: Types and Tips

SO WHO ARE THESE MEN—these fit, firm, full of life, and hotter than a chili pepper specimens just waiting for a like-minded cougar to come along? They're everyone—and everywhere. An experienced cougar will have her preferred hunting grounds, and will know—before moving in for the kill—the pros and cons associated with different species. For the uninitiated, however, what follows is a guide to the most common types of prey, along with some helpful hunting tips.

The Millennium Man

FORMERLY KNOWN AS the New Age Man, this prey is kind, sensitive, loving, romantic, aware, intelligent, generous, open-minded, artistic, and into faithfulness. In other words, he's too good to be true. Nevertheless, every cougar dreams of finding one, and suffers major disappointment with each failed effort. Unfortunately, there are only one or two of these cats in the jungle.

The Millennium Man will probably be deeply disillusioned about life. He's been used, misused, and abused by just about everyone, including cougars if they're given half a chance. A smart cougar will somehow resist the temptation to embark on a feeding frenzy, and simply enjoy the sheer pleasure of dating such a gentle soul—at least until she finds out what's wrong with him.

If you're hunting for a guy with money, prestige, and his own car, this is not the one. He's too sensitive and kind to make big money or have a powerful career. He does love to bond, though, so he may press you to meet his parents early on. What's worse, he may want you to be friends with his ex-wife or his last two girlfriends, all of whom he adores and talks to at least twice a day on the phone.

He's a seeker of spirituality, which means that he's into either a cult or an alternative religion. When the moon is full, you might find him dancing and chanting on your condo balcony. Don't be surprised if he takes his smudge pot around the bedroom to clear bad vibrations before you perform The Great Rite. He's likely to be searching for his inner soul through meditation or channeling, and will know how to read tarot cards. He'll own a well-worn video of *The Sixth Sense* and may have an obsessive compulsive personality. This is fine, as long as it's your needs he's obsessive about.

He'll fall quickly, deeply in love and may want to father your child. Tell him it's your karma to remain childless (at least from now on). If you continue the relationship, he will want emotional support and will certainly return it in spades. This is a man who isn't afraid to cry, hug, or tell people he loves them.

He may drink too much or smoke pot when he can afford it. This is okay—you do, too. Visa will call him regularly about his huge credit card debt. Older men will think he's a wimp. Older women will adore him. Your friends will find him a curiosity. He may grow on you.

ADVANTAGES AND DISADVANTAGES

Y He believes in commitment, which is usually a shock to the commitment-phobic cougar.

Y He'll be great in bed. (Every cougar knows that this is where kindness, sensitivity, love, and romance really count.)

COUGAR PREY: TYPES AND TIPS

- ♈ He'll always be squeaky clean. (You'll have to shave before each encounter.)
- ♈ He'll ask you if you've been tested for HIV, but will be genuinely surprised and possibly offended when you ask the same.
- ♈ He may be a good cook, but will probably be vegetarian or vegan. This will drive you crazy in restaurants; expect to feel guilt over ordering a steak.
- ♈ He'll love animals and will be a fount of knowledge as to what plants will grow in the dusty, empty pots on your balcony or patio.
- ♈ He believes in sharing everything—especially your money.

WHERE TO HUNT

You won't find a Millennium Man at your local bar's Cougar Night. Instead, check out libraries, bookstores, lectures and workshops on spiritual subjects, gardening clubs and centers, yoga and Tai Chi classes, occult stores, symphony or ancient music concerts, and museum events. Attract his attention by telling him you see dead people, have had three previous lives (be sure to know when and where they were and don't be boring and say you were Cleopatra), or that your aunt is a Wiccan High Priestess. Read a number of Shirley MacLaine books.

The Techie

IN MANY WAYS, the Techie is like a Millennium Man—from a different planet. He knows more about computers, the Internet, virtual reality camcorders, all things digital, cell phones and videophones, electronic games, robotics, artificial intelligence, lasers, and space sound recording than you could ever dream of knowing. Most cougars feel that the techie world has already reached its zenith—they can, after all, shop on the Internet.

Although the Techie ages like everyone else, you'd never know it. He's still blissfully mesmerized by the latest video game or new hand-held technological miracle, and prying him away from a computer is like unsticking Crazy Glue. This can be a real challenge for the cougar wanting to stretch her body rather than her mind. In fact, the Techie is often so absorbed and stimulated by his own complex world that the act of "plugging in" can be downright orgasmic. Daunting competition.

The Techie unplugged

Sexually, the Techie likes masturbation and oral sex—both leave a hand free to move the mouse. He may have voice-activated computer equipment and may occasionally bark commands during sex. Make sure you activate. He may be hooked on Internet sites with dubious titles such as "Underage Nude Nymphos." The Techie often considers on-line porn the perfect form of sex—it's all in one spot and he doesn't have to leave his computer to get it. It also means that he doesn't have to relate to real women, whom he finds demanding and annoying because they can't be switched off.

ADVANTAGES AND DISADVANTAGES

- ☖ You'll never have to call a technical support service while you're dating him, and your friends and relatives will think he's great (he'll help them out for free, too).
- ☖ He'll write constantly to you via e-mail and will expect you to reply. This is fine—e-mail is faster and cheaper than snail mail or cell phones.
- ☖ He may insist on installing a computer station that NASA would be proud of at your home and then dash to it the minute he arrives. He could sit there for two days unless

you do something drastic such as pulling the plug. (A subtle reminder that this is not why he's visiting you.)

Y He'll expect you to show some interest in his world. Tell him that you certainly know the difference between "floppy" and "hard."

Y He'll drive you crazy at movies by telling you—detail by minute detail—how the special effects were done, even if you're convinced that the dinosaurs are real.

Y He'll love techno music. You'll hate it.

Y He might be a dot.com millionaire, although you'd never know it by his clothes. He usually looks like an unmade and (occasionally) unwashed bed.

WHERE TO HUNT

Another type you won't find at the bars. Try computer super-stores, shows and conventions, chat rooms or dating websites, video game and DVD sections of stores, or your city's version of Silicon Valley. Invest in the latest hand-held computer or laptop and flash it around. Dress all in black. If you're really serious, stop wearing makeup and washing your hair. He'll gravitate automatically as he'll think you're a Techie, too.

34

COUGAR PREY: TYPES AND TIPS

The Overly Ambitious Professional

A TOUGH YOUNG MAN for a cougar to land—mainly because he'll think that an older woman might not be good for his career. He's right in that you certainly have no intention of ever playing corporate wifey again. But youthful ambition can be an alluring scent.

On the other hand, he'll certainly be willing prey if you are successful or rich—he worships both attributes with a driven fervor. Driving a Merc or a Beemer is also an asset; ditto for looking like an extra from *Traders*. If you happen to be his boss, he's yours.

OAPs are very impressed by designer labels and luxury goods, so dig out your best Chanel bag, Hermes scarf, and Cartier watch, even if they're knockoffs. Know the names of all the latest trendy restaurants—especially the ones that choose who they let in—even if you've never set foot inside. Talk about the volatility of the tech stock market and how glad you are that you've always followed Warren Buffett. (Never mind if you secretly think he's a singer from the '60s.)

He'll like sex as long as it doesn't take too much of his valuable time. Squeezing it into his busy schedule—which includes long hours at work, at the gym, on the cell phone and on the laptop; squash games; visits to his therapist; checking the stock market; and reading the financial newspapers and latest How to Succeed books—can be a challenge. Despite his ambition at work, he'll want you to initiate sex; he's always too exhausted.

ADVANTAGES AND DISADVANTAGES

- ♈ He's paranoid about sexual diseases, so he'll be faithful to you until he meets someone who's richer or more successful.

- ♈ He'll always be well dressed, just in case he runs into his boss.

- ♈ His gifts will all come with designer labels, even if they were actually made by six year olds in Bangladesh.

- ♈ He'll love the fact that you're not interested in marriage, kids, or living together—all of which would take too much time away from his upward climb.

- ♈ He'll give you good investment tips. Watch out if they turn out to be too good. He could be insider trading, in which case he might not be around for too long.

- ♈ He makes a good accessory for the image-conscious cougar. (Make sure you get the real thing, cheap imitations won't do.)

Where to Hunt

Trendy coffee shops, restaurants and bars, the finance section of big bookstores, the city's financial district and all peripheral eating places and watering holes, spas (he's de-stressing), upscale gyms, seminars on success or investing. Dress sexily but with quality for this one.

The Jock

GOOD PREY IF you want to get fit fast. Brush the dust off your tennis racquet, pull out your jogging shoes, and get ready to play. Don't be surprised, though, if he just wants you to watch. This has more to do with narcissism than sex. You may end up standing at the edge of a wet, muddy field or sitting in a freezing hockey rink while he "performs." You'll also be expected to nurse his wounds afterward.

Don't pounce unless you're in reasonably good shape. Jocks are very body-obsessed, although he'll likely be more interested in his own than in yours. He may spend hours at the gym (pumping iron) and in front of the mirror (checking his six-pack abs). Always oblige when he says "feel this." If he is the body beautiful type, he'll be a much-envied companion who will make other cougars snarl with jealousy. If he's not, why are you hunting him?

ADVANTAGES AND DISADVANTAGES

- When it comes to sex, he will either have wonderful athletic ability or be uselessly speedy and selfish. (The competitive drive to "finish first" can travel from the running track to the bedroom.)

- He won't offer anything in the way of intellectual conversation, and if you want to animate him, you may have to read and quote from the sports section for the first time in your life.

- He could turn out to be an armchair jock who endlessly watches sports on television. You'll end up adding pounds as you sit there eating chips and drinking beer.

- He'll never have sex before The Big Game. It's too weakening and may be prohibited by his contract.

- He'll never go to a symphony concert or an art show, and since persuading a Jock to give up his baseball hat (worn backward, of course) is like asking Hugh Hefner to give up sex, you may as well put the cultural side of life aside while dating this guy.

 ⅄ He'll entertain your kids. This is great—unless your teenage daughter gets the urge to exercise with him.

WHERE TO HUNT

Sports events, health clubs, gyms, hockey arenas, sports bars, tennis clubs, parks with sports areas, beaches, and boardwalks. Wear sporty sunglasses, athletic-style clothes, and beat-up sneakers (Jocks sneer at new ones). Always carry a bottle of water and a sports bag bearing some sort of logo. If you want to be sure of his undivided attention, just wear your sleaziest outfit.

The Environmental Activist

PERFECT IF YOU'RE feeling guilty (perish the thought) about pouncing on younger men. You can tell yourself you're doing your bit for the planet. Like others who are Into Causes, he'll be passionate, sensitive, aware, and totally unable to see anyone else's point of view. He may be vegetarian or vegan and will undoubtedly have strong views on issues such as fur trapping and factory farming.

You may have to alter your eating and household habits. The Activist will react badly to meat, white bread and sugar, bleach, paper towels, plastic wrap, leather, and pesticides—all of which you can't live without. He'll deeply disapprove of air conditioning, even though it's a necessity if you've reached menopause. He'll react negatively to your gas-guzzling SUV—or any car for that matter—but he'll like riding in it if it's luxurious. He may even consider running water to be a luxury. Show him how showering together can conserve water and be fun.

He might be into such horrors as outdoor camping or sex in wild, prickly, and mosquito-ridden spots in the Great Outdoors. Try to divert him to the Great Indoors. Use green sheets on your bed and fill the room with potted plants.

Advantages and Disadvantages

♈ He'll make you more aware and (maybe) responsible about the desperately beleaguered natural world around you— even if your idea of reduce, reuse, and recycle is going on a diet, using a paper tissue twice, and buying a secondhand Hermes bag on eBay.

Y He'll love all animals and insects (hide your collection of Raid products) and will treat your cats like real people. He'll be the rare young man who doesn't mind them staring at you while you make love.

Y He may talk to trees and plants and get your one orchid to finally bloom.

Y He'll want to go for long hikes in the rain and attend protest rallies. The latter is fun for cougars only if they don't get arrested.

WHERE TO HUNT

Be on the lookout for anyone wearing canvas shoes, a t-shirt with a save-something-or-another message on it, and a hug-a-tree-today pin. You'll find him in vegetarian restaurants, organic food stores, at protest marches and rallies, seminars on environmental issues, and conservation areas. He won't attend a Cougar Night and he may not drink alcohol (scary thought), although he might consider wine "natural" and drink copious quantities, especially if you're paying. Wear natural fibers, talk composting, and tell him you've met David Suzuki.

The Intellectual

THE INTELLECTUAL CAN be interesting prey and is welcome relief if you've just finished dating a Jock. He hates sports and pales visibly when faced with sports equipment. He might be a musician, artist, student, computer techie, or mowing your lawn to earn money for his meditative hike through Kathmandu.

He won't have any money, but he may have a weakness for drugs and booze. He won't mind at all if you use your money to pay for them. He may be expensive in the long run. He'll prefer art movies to Hollywood pics. If the art movies leave you completely confused, he'll happily spend hours explaining them in excruciating detail.

Intellectuals are often great in bed. With any luck, he'll consider Tantric sex and the multiple orgasm as the ultimate ways to raise his level of consciousness—and yours, too.

ADVANTAGES AND DISADVANTAGES

Y He'll introduce you to your city's most obscure art galleries and artists, and will encourage you to accompany him to concerts and poetry readings.

- ꭩ He'll know exactly where your G-spot is and call all your parts by their correct names.
- ꭩ His conversation will always be stimulating. As this can often be tiring, he may not be the best companion after dark or after a hard day at work.
- ꭩ He will stun into silence even the most aggressive and educated of your friends with his knowledge of the supremely obscure.
- ꭩ He may consider sex a bestial act and a waste of time.
- ꭩ He will undoubtedly fall madly in love with you and might convince you that he's your soulmate.

WHERE TO HUNT

Art galleries, symphony concerts, poetry readings, cultural events, bookstores, wine stores, bars (he's the one nursing a single drink all evening), university campuses, computer stores and shows, Tantric workshops, and sex seminars. He likes classic clothes. Wear rimless glasses and look earnest.

The Divorced/Separated/ Split-from-Cohabitation

IF YOU'RE HUNTING in the over-thirty set, this is by far the largest category of prey. Unlike older Divorceds, Separated, or Splits, the younger variety has usually had only one partner, meaning there's a lot less baggage being carried around. The drawback is that his ex is often hovering in the background and dominating his conversation. She'll also dominate your phone with unpleasant calls if she finds out about you. (Young women often go into angry shock upon hearing that their ex is with an older woman.)

He may have one or two children about whom he feels terribly guilty. He will want to bring them to your place on his access weekend, where they'll proceed to wreck the furniture, scare the cat, and empty the fridge. He'll be constantly in debt as he's overloaded with alimony payments, lawyer's fees, school fees, and his guilty need to buy the kids expensive gifts.

He'll spend more time on his therapist's couch than in your bed, or you'll end up being his therapist for free. He'll endlessly tell you How Much It All Cost, What Went Wrong, and What She Did to Me. He'll insist that he isn't bitter. He'll be constantly on his cell phone either having a fight with her or talking to the kids. When drunk, he'll say he's thinking of going back to her for the sake of the kids. He'll want to know what you think. He may want you to do his laundry.

ADVANTAGES AND DISADVANTAGES

🍸 He'll be totally housebroken and may even cook—a big benefit for cougars whose idea of a meal is one that comes with a check.

🍸 He'll be used to frequent sex.

🍸 He might be handy around the house or apartment.

🍸 He won't mind grocery shopping and will love staying at home in front of the fire.

🍸 He'll enjoy wild nights on the town, since they never happened when he was attached. (Make sure you're with him.)

🍸 He won't have to be educated about PMS, fat days, or the fact that you may not look your best first thing in the morning.

🍸 He'll love your sports car—driving one was a dream when he was attached.

45

☥ He'll love the fact you don't want a commitment, but may not stick around long. Statistics show he'll probably end up marrying again and having more kids.

WHERE TO HUNT

Cougar Nights at bars, all nights at bars, night clubs, health clubs, therapists' and lawyers' offices, alone with kids at fast food outlets on Sunday (it's his access weekend), any place catering to kids' activities (ditto), apartment elevators (he's renting the Post-Divorce bachelor pad). You'll also meet him at friends' parties and dinners as they're trying to match him (or you) up with Someone Special. Tell him you've just come out of a bad relationship and he'll be yours for the entire evening. It will take him that long to tell you about his breakup. He'll love your sexy clothes as his ex never wore such stuff. But if you get into a long-term situation, he'll want you to stop wearing them.

The Gay

YOU MAY THINK THAT *Will & Grace* is far-fetched, but cougars know it isn't. Many have gay friends, and some have even dated or married gays either by mistake or arrangement.

The problem in most big cities? If he's clean, handsome, well-dressed, well-mannered, and single, he's most likely gay.

The Gay loves cougars—as dates or friends. This is an asset for all concerned: neither needs to worry about what will happen at the end of an evening awash in too much wine. (Any cougar who considers sex to be the tastiest part of the hunt should look elsewhere.) The Gay will encourage you to share secrets you've never told anyone else. Steel yourself for the lurid details of his intricate and overwrought love life and the fact that you will find out who among your own friends and acquaintances is really gay.

He may have expensive habits and too many clothes. He may be obsessively neat and a wizard in the kitchen. He may want to borrow your clothes and redesign your home several times a year. You will have to share him with his gay dates and endure very late, very emotional calls when his latest relationship turns rocky—usually after the second date.

ADVANTAGES AND DISADVANTAGES

- ▼ He will always be well dressed (unless he's into the macho leather look).
- ▼ He'll help you choose your clothes (usually over-the-top and sexually flamboyant).

- ⚲ He'll never expect a French kiss, although he will want lots of hugs.
- ⚲ He'll urge you to stick with your fitness program, not because a fit woman's body is exciting to him but because he intensely dislikes flab and fat on anyone.
- ⚲ He'll be very supportive and sympathetic when you're having a Bad Day (as long as he's not having one, too) or temper tantrum. He knows a lot about both.
- ⚲ He won't be demanding of your time—he, too, has his Other Life.
- ⚲ Your girlfriend won't want to steal him.

WHERE TO HUNT

Big cities, or any event connected to fashion, show business, television, hair styling, or interior design. Gyms, health clubs, bars (gay, of course), furnishing and fitness stores, fresh food markets and delicatessens, classy menswear stores, working in restaurants or behind bars (between acting gigs). Definitely won't be at Cougar Night. Flamboyance is the key in what you wear. The Gay likes women with life and style. He likes men who have it far better.

The Ethnic

GLOBAL VILLAGE, MULTICULTURALISM, melting pot—whatever the concept, it means that the cougar has a greater variety of prey. Unfortunately, many of these cultures have very strong ideas about appropriate relationships for their young men. Older women—WASP or ethnic—are not in any of the approved categories. This isn't a bad thing. You'll never have to meet his family (unless it's in a threatening, dark-alley situation).

He won't like it if you have preconceived notions about his nationality. If you think they're all nutso drivers or totally dominated by their mothers you may want to stop before you start. He might not like being asked when he immigrated to your country. He was probably born here.

Dating the Ethnic will guarantee a crash course in his native geography, customs, foods, and beverages. To him, these will always be far finer than anything anyone else offers, especially you. He may have some disconcerting customs regarding sex. If he says prayers before getting into bed and insists that it face east, view it as enlightening. It's still better than watching National Geographic programs on the television.

COUGAR PREY: TYPES AND TIPS

ADVANTAGES AND DISADVANTAGES

- Y He may appear extraordinarily attractive when he's young. The fact he can turn into a very unattractive older man shouldn't bother you—you're hunting only for the short term.

- Y He'll expand your knowledge and your sexual repertoire. Many cultures have some unusual and ancient ideas about how to excite a woman. They're often right.

- Y He won't want to marry you or live with you, but he will be passionately devoted to you in a way that men of your own ethnic background won't understand.

- Y He'll be your own personal guide if you visit his country or island of origin. He'll teach you to drink copious amounts of his potent and foul-tasting national beverage without falling under the table.

- Y You will hate his music and he will hate yours.

WHERE TO HUNT

Ethnic restaurants and bars, cultural events, university campuses, adult education classes, and government offices. He will certainly attend Cougar Nights (never underestimate the allure

COUGAR PREY: TYPES AND TIPS

of The Forbidden). Tell him how interesting his country and its history are even if you don't have a clue where to find it on a map. If he's from the Middle East, never mention politics, women's liberation, or the price of oil. But feel free to show him exactly what liberated women do and want. Wear anything plunging or high cut.

The Still Married

BAD COUGAR.

Yes, I know it's hard to spot this particular prey, especially if he's not wearing a ring. But smart cougars always ask about availability—preferably before sex. Whiskers should quiver if he goes home every night at the same hour, if he's always leaving restaurant tables to make private phone calls, or if he's unavailable on weekends and holidays. Whiskers should be playing Beethoven's Fifth if he also makes excuses about giving out his home address or phone number. Most cougars will flick their tails and walk away. Others may sniff the alluring and often addictive scent of illicit subterfuge and follow it—with their eyes wide open, of course.

ADVANTAGES AND DISADVANTAGES

- ☙ He won't make any demands, but you can't make any either.
- ☙ He may give you his best, and take his worst home to someone else.
- ☙ He won't be looking for anything long term.
- ☙ You may have to wear a bulletproof vest if his wife finds out.

WHERE TO HUNT

Try not to. Getting embroiled in the Eternal Triangle is an exercise in never-ending frustration. It's also often a waste of time—a precious commodity cougars don't like to waste, especially on emotions that can end up mangled in a trash compactor. If you simply can't resist, fasten your seat belt. You're in for a trip that's akin to bungee jumping without a cord.

The Generation Gap

ALTHOUGH **MOST** cougars are confident, stylish hunters who are always sure of their prey, unexpected problems can crop up from time to time. Most are the result of the generation gap—known in modern-speak as the intergenerational gap. Although the gap can be small enough to step across, it can also be a bottomless abyss. The size of both the gap and the problems it causes are dependent upon two things: background and age difference.

If your prey is six to eight years younger, there should be only a minor chasm; if the age difference is in the ten-to-twenty-year range, you could find yourself facing an alien species. Always up for a challenge, cougars will think positively. At worst, the encounter will be a learning experience; at best, it's an easy way to re-enter a vibrant, often weird, youthful world without going through regressive therapy.

Use sex as a bridge and take heart; most of what follows applies only when the relationship lasts more than a couple of very hot nights. Of course, this explains why most cougars choose to limit their encounters to a couple of very hot nights.

There are hundreds of areas in which the generation gap tends to appear. Here are a few of the most common.

Computers

DON'T EVEN TRY to compete or be fully aware of the latest innovations in this field unless you're a computer whiz and know more than him anyway. Most cougars are familiar with and often very skillful on a computer. They may use one daily and occasionally make forays onto the Internet for information and good shopping. They are not obsessed. Many young men are. They spend inordinate amounts of time surfing, hacking, or just listening to their colored whiz machine talk. As far as a cougar is concerned, any obsession that isn't focused on her is a waste of good leisure time. Look on him as a personal service provider and make sure he provides the service where it counts.

Electronic Gadgets

AGAIN, DON'T EVEN try to keep up with the latest. Let your younger man do that for you. You may think that "wireless" is an old-fashioned radio, or feel you're doing just fine with your cell phone, electronic diary, and wafer-thin laptop. He'll tell you how out of date they (and you) are, and will be full of suggestions as to what you should buy to replace them. (As I have mentioned before, dating younger men can be expensive.) He may be constantly glued to his cell phone or Palm Pilot. As your wish is to be connected to *his* palm, which you will then pilot, you should divert his attention with some tried-and-true technology of your own. Try bare flesh.

(Note: The limited length of the previous two items is intentional. I'm told I'm a techno-phobe because I'm not fully comfortable with anything that beeps and talks but doesn't need a washroom. After all, I come from an era that predated microwave ovens, computers, paper towels, and ballpoint pens; an era when "digital" was something you did with your finger. As a young journalist, I used a manual typewriter! Despite having learned what I think is an amazing amount of tolerance for today's technology, my VCR still flashes. I intend for the next younger man in my life to fix it. Then I'll fix him.)

Television

YOUR YOUNG MAN probably grew up with his eyes glued to the television. He feels comfortable with it blaring in the background and may want it on all the time, even when he's not watching. He'll want you to have a digital, big-screen model and every package the cable company can offer so he can choose from 250 channels. Then he'll say there's nothing worth watching. He won't like *Ally McBeal* or National Geographic specials. Since his attention span will undoubtedly be far shorter than yours, divert him with something real and exciting—like oral sex. Make sure he puts down the remote first.

Music

ONE OF THE GREAT satisfactions in music for anyone older these days is the renewed fascination with the oldies and goldies you knew and loved as a kid. Your man may consider the top stars of the '60s and '70s geriatric, but they're definitely jumping, jiving, and wailing again. You'll be considered totally awesome if you own anything original by the Beatles, actually saw Elvis in concert, met Mick Jagger (far better if you slept with him), or were a groupie with the Boomtown Rats. Despite all this, the music gap will be wide if you hate rap and rave and think The Barenaked Ladies are a strip show. Try making love to classical music—especially Ravel's "Bolero," which was used in the sex scene between Bo Derek and Dudley Moore in the movie *10*. If he's not old enough to remember, you're dating too young.

Clubs

BACK IN YOUR DAY, clubs were probably discos lit by brightly colored lights and pulsating beams. They were cheerful places where everyone danced, chatted, and mingled. Welcome to the millennium nightlife—or nitelife, as it's now called. Clubs are huge, almost completely blacked-out, cavernous places where the guys wear black (so you can't see them) and the young women are close to stark naked. The sound is so loud your breastbone jumps, your ears pop, and you need sign language to communicate with anyone, including the bartenders. Everyone looks miserable, no one seems to dance with anyone else, and the average age seems to be about fourteen. Your younger man will love it. A better bet for the sophisticated cougar who doesn't want to damage her ears is to show him some private dance moves that feature two bodies pressed tightly together.

Movies

THE MOVIE GAP is actually more of a male/female difference than a generation gap. You like chick flicks (featuring strong, cougar-style women, of course) and Merchant Ivory and Jane Austen features that move at half speed. He'll refuse to see them no matter what sexual favors you offer. What he wants to see is at least seven people violently murdered and dismembered, four car chases, three buildings blown to smithereens, and a couple of sickening rapes—preferably in the first half hour. He'll have seen the *Blair Witch* movies twice and will rave about *American Psycho*'s brilliance. He'll never have heard of *Citizen Kane* and may ask if Ben Affleck was in it. Try renting old classics (young men love Humphrey Bogart) and showing him what he *can't* get at a movie complex.

Food

FOOD WILL BE a passion with your latest prey. The problem is that his idea of food is "fast"—burgers, fries, fried chicken, subs, and pizza, washed down with cola, beer, or coolers, and followed by a candy bar. Just watching him eat is guaranteed to bring a cougar out in a rash and put an immediate ten pounds on her hips. He won't have a clue about the fit-for-life diet or nouvelle cuisine. He won't care about calories, fat grams, or the carb-to-protein ratio. The only greenery he'll eat will be the salad that automatically comes with his massive steak or double burger. But good cougars never nag—tell him to "eat his vegetables" and you'll remind him of his mother. If you're lucky, he'll love candlelight dinners and gourmet food. Show him that the way to a cougar's heart is through good reservations. Then, rent *9½ Weeks* and show him exactly what can be done with two bodies and food.

Jewelry

NOT YOURS—HIS. Male jewelry, especially via piercing, is a contemporary fashion that truly divides the older woman from

Magnetic appeal

the younger man. A cougar tends to believe that jewelry is for the adornment of women, not men. While she was growing up, the only men wearing earrings were starring in fantasy pirate movies. However, she might consider a man with a link bracelet or neck chain progressive. Clearly, he's comfortable with his feminine side. Chances are good that he's also quite comfortable with multiple piercings and pieces of decorative metal—in the most private and unusual parts of his anatomy. If he fails to mention this, you might find yourself unexpectedly crunching upon some trinket or another during sensual exploration. This is when a body massage before sexual contact can be so informative. Tattoos can be just as eye-widening and annoying, especially if they include a woman's name that isn't his mother's. Try to find a young man who thinks, like you, that jewelry looks adorable on women. Encourage him to buy it for you frequently.

Clothes

YOUNG MEN ARE divided into two groups—those into the latest street stuff and those who dress more conservatively, mostly for business purposes. It's usually an age thing—the younger the man, the more hip the clothes. This can mean pants that droop so much the crotch is at his knees. Resist the impulse to reach over and pull them up. Everything he wears will be so baggy you won't be able to tell if he's thin or overweight. He may wear his sneakers untied. Again, resist. You may want to go out and buy his clothes. Unlike older men, he'll eagerly let you do this, especially if you're paying. Be prepared to take earplugs—without them, your hearing could be irreversibly damaged by the store's "background" music. If you like his clothes, he won't mind a bit if you want to borrow them, but they may not have seen the inside of a washing machine for a long time. Proceed with caution if he wants to borrow yours.

A big plus with young men is their underwear. Most wear great (read "minuscule") underwear. Some wear none at all. In this case he's either the most sensual find of the year or he hasn't done a wash in months. Another pleasure with young men and clothes? Many love to be without them. They have absolutely no inhibitions and love to walk around the house naked. He'll expect you to do the same, which can be a hazard if the door bell rings or your neighbor pops by unexpectedly.

Your young man will hate wearing a full suit and tie (unless he's in that overly ambitious category). He'll downright dread donning a tuxedo. Under severe pressure, he will go out and rent one for a gala evening, especially if you're paying for the $250 tickets. Be prepared to melt at the sight of him. A tuxedo will make him look even younger and even better. Ignore anyone who asks if he's your son or the waiter.

Vacations

PLANNING A VACATION with your young man can quickly illuminate the gap. Cougars who lead hectic lives dream of an exotic place where they can lie half-naked under an umbrella on a hot, sandy beach, sipping a drink that looks like a bunch of flowers and reading a book. In this dream, the evening would be spent leisurely dining under the stars, taking a long walk on the sand, and enjoying a potent nightcap or two (or more) at the bar.

Young men also dream of exotic places. His fantasy, however, involves going completely naked on a hot, sandy beach where rock music blasts out of five massive speakers. He'll imagine drinking beer out of cans and tossing back so many flower drinks that he passes out face down on the beach. His ideal evening would be spent in a dark disco (after grabbing something at the buffet) where five more massive speakers blast out more rock. He will like your idea of potent drinks at the bar but will return to the room only when the morning light appears. He'll then sleep all day, wake up, and want sex.

He'll adamantly refuse to go on tours (most young men find ruins boring), preferring to ruin himself at the pool bar. This can, in turn, ruin you when you get the toilet-roll-style bill at the end of your stay. Of course, it's great if you're dating a young man who shares your interests and needs, but since few young men can stay in one place for long, the vacationing cougar should have stamina and a large capacity for booze. Luckily, a cougar wouldn't be a cougar if she didn't have copious amounts of the first and enjoy copious amounts of the second.

No matter how big the generation gap is or how difficult a cougar might find her prey's youthful habits and alien lifestyle, all is not lost. You both have a couple of traits in common, and I've found that they overcome just about everything. Your raging libidos and overwhelming lust for each other will get you through. As Confucius said, lust is the Great Leveler. (Actually, he didn't. That's my thought.)

What a Cougar Wants, a Cougar Gets

WHILE PREY DOES indeed come in many ages, shapes, sizes, and income brackets, cougars generally pounce on younger men for one reason and one reason only. It has nothing to do with money, ego, marriage, children, a mothering instinct, a desire to explore his mind, or the urge to use him as an accessory. (Okay, maybe as an accessory. There's far more cachet in having a young hunk on your arm than a Chanel or Prada bag.) There's really no prize for guessing. The main attraction is—you knew it all along—sex!

But the uninformed think (and often say) that a younger man couldn't possibly be interested in sex with an older woman when plenty of women in his own age pack are ready, willing, and able. As usual, the uninformed couldn't be more wrong.

Unlike a younger woman, the older woman understands the benefits of good sex. This is the direct result of having experienced too much of the bad stuff with older or same-age men. An older woman knows that sex feels good, is stimulating, is good exercise, and helps to release tension, keep her skin clear, and diminish wrinkles. She knows that it makes her feel young and puts a happy smile on her face. She knows that it may help keep arthritis and osteoporosis at bay. She knows—beyond a shadow of a doubt—that sex is far more exciting and palatable than apple cider vinegar tablets.

If the cougar's in-depth knowledge of the many benefits of sex isn't enough to interest the younger man, he need only consider the following:

A COUGAR WILL ...

Y be enthusiastic and skilled in the sexual arts

Y carry her own condoms

Y initiate oral sex and expect it to be reciprocated—often

Y demonstrate imaginative and creative sexual moves—the kind he's only read about in men's magazines

Y introduce him to a level of sensuality he didn't know existed

- always have accessories ready—candles, matches, tissues, lubrication, massage oils, incense, sex toys, handcuffs, silk ropes, and chilled wine. (Handcuffs? Silk rope? Heck, why not?)
- wear the sexiest lingerie Victoria's Secret has to offer
- know the power and effect of wearing just a smile
- have an intelligent conversation afterward

A Cougar Won't ...

- wince when oral sex is suggested
- use sex as a manipulation or a weapon
- want to be introduced to the family—ever
- want to introduce him to her family—if they're still alive
- get pregnant—ever
- ask when she's going to see him again

Delivering the Goods

ONCE A COUGAR has landed her prey, she has to deliver. And having delivered, she has to keep it up—at least if she intends to keep him for a while. A young man, having discovered the bound-

Never say "not now"

less joys of cougar sex, will be able to think of only two things—sex and more sex. So if your idea of frequent sex is once a week, and only if you haven't been to the hair stylist in the last couple of days, forget younger men. If you like to plan ahead or set a regular time and place, give up your whiskers and become a stud mare.

Younger men love the sexually unexpected; the urge will sweep over them while barbecuing hot dogs, buying athletic shoes, or browsing in the frozen food section of the supermarket. Your prey can turn hunter while you're loading the dishwasher, heading to work, cleaning your teeth, or pulling up weeds in the garden. Cougars never, ever say "not now."

But as much as a cougar loves sex, she also has A Life. (Even though older men are often stating otherwise.) This means that much as she would love to spend every day steaming under the sheets, soaking up good wine and even better sex, there are pressing matters to consider. She's got to claw her way up the corporate ladder, take care of pesky household chores, tend to family demands and, most importantly, leave time for personal pleasure and grooming.

Saying "no" while whetting his appetite for "when" can take organizational skills that would make even the indomitable

Martha Stewart blanch. So, if a heavy duty case of the wilts appear to be sweeping in, a smart cougar demonstrates that sex is part of a full and fascinating life that includes conversation, meals (out, if possible), books, music, movies, trips, parties and, if really stymied, walks together. This will all prove to be a wonderful education (the government should really devise a generous Cougar Grant to subsidize these efforts), but despite the cougar's best efforts, the besotted young man will still want only one thing. Any guesses?

The Fine Art of Seduction

BEING AS SMART and sophisticated as she is, the cougar often prefers a single sexual encounter. Anything more takes too much time, effort, and commitment. (Cougars are not into commitment.) If, however, a cougar finds herself stalking particularly tasty prey—prey that she might want to savor for more than one night—it's worth remembering a few pointers. A cougar may be used to sex with older men. Sex with younger men is a whole new ballgame.

Helpful Reminders

- Y Younger men use the correct names for private parts. Older men have slang names that they use as swear words or growl at you through clenched teeth at the moment of climax.

- Y Younger men are relaxed about orgasms. They want you to have one but if you don't, it's okay. Older men think it's all your own fault.

- Y Younger men will ask you to show them what it takes to help you have an orgasm. Older men won't bother: they think it's demeaning, and besides, they've already had one, so what's the point?

- Y Younger men may, when confronted with the reality of all their wet dreams, be a little hasty. This is infinitely preferable to slogging away for hours on a flagging older libido.

- Y Younger men are sometimes nervous during the first encounter. They may have had too much to drink, and may not be at their best. To be fair, most cougars prefer to have had a few drinks themselves. Hunting cats know their skills are honed to perfection by a few straight-up martinis.

Okay, so you've picked him up and taken him home. Or perhaps you haven't pounced yet. Whatever the situation, you've clearly decided he's worthy prey. You'd like nothing more than to take him home and show him your claws—and everything else. At this point, you should already have your quarry panting with anticipation. When you first encountered him—at the bar, on the dance floor, or in the produce section—you were probably crystal clear about what you had in mind. (Think Sharon Stone in *Basic Instinct*.) Now, you need to proceed to the next step. A seduction may be in order.

Invite him back to your place—on another day if possible. Going back to his place that night is, of course, an option. It all depends on your level of lust and his address. If it's snobby—and suggests the presence of a weekly cleaning lady—you may want to pounce sooner rather than later.

Next, plan a meal. No, I'm not going to say that the way to a man's heart is through his stomach. Cougars know exactly how to reach a man's heart, and it has nothing to do with food. The meal is a simple necessity: there's no pleasure in landing starving prey. Now, don't panic. The meal doesn't have to be gourmet or even cooked from scratch. (Most cougars have long since replaced the "must-be-fresh" approach with "ready-to-heat-unrecognizable-gourmet" from the nearby market.) The major items on your shopping list should be pretty basic: plenty of wine, beer (or whatever you both like to drink), and condoms.

While the beverage of choice is chilling, you can set the scene. Light the candles and the fireplace. (Only if it's winter. You don't want to sweat yet.) Cue up some appropriate music, and gather the necessary accessories (see page 67). No time to clean up and the house is a mess? Leave the lights off and bundle him into the bedroom by candlelight, hoping all the while that the sheets aren't rumpled and that those piles of used underwear are somewhere out of sight.

Pouncing with Panache

OCCASIONALLY, YOU MAY find that your young prey is nervous—especially if it's his first time with an older, more experienced woman. It's a rare occurrence, but one for which a good cougar should be prepared. It may be up to you to make all of the moves. Help him out of his coat. Fill him with food and wine. Then get close and intimate.

If things are progressing more slowly than you'd like, an honest approach usually does the trick. Blunt words—"wanna make love?"—often have an amazing effect. Most young men will be visibly relieved that you're taking the lead. If your latest prey isn't, and is already firmly planted on the couch with a beer in one hand and the remote in the other, you're hunting in the wrong part of the jungle. Unlock the cage and send him home.

It's much more likely, though, that he'll jump at your offer. For most young men, the mere hint of impending sex will lead to an automatic erection. At that point, nothing short of an earthquake or a call from his mother will change the mood.

Now, despite the fact that most cougars are supremely self-confident, there isn't an older woman on earth who doesn't have at least one quarrel with her body. And in this crucial pre-pounce moment, concerns regarding shape, size, or lack of firmness might just sneak through the martini fumes. Try not to think twice. Very few men—especially young men—concern themselves with figure flaws when the promise of sex is dangling like the proverbial carrot. It might also help to remember that a man who has experienced life-altering sex—which your prey is about to do—never talks about figure faults when questioned.

He'll recall his partner's passion, skill, and enthusiasm. He'll go on *ad nauseam* about the sheer pleasure of being with someone so relaxed and confident in the bedroom. The word "cellulite" will never even cross his mind, no less his lips. Total sexual satisfaction is, after all, blind.

If you're still nervous, remember that nothing hides flaws better than candlelight.

The Cougar in Action

MY MOST RECENT seduction involved a man ten years younger than me. I'd been interested for ages, but I took my time before making a move. Stalking prey takes careful maneuvering and a lot of patience—especially if the prey smells danger. But I knew that careful persistence would eventually pay off. (I do, after all, have the honed instincts of a practiced, long-time cougar.) This was one prey that wanted to be caught!

Experience had demonstrated that he liked being in my company, laughed at my jokes, openly appraised what I was wearing, asked my opinion too often, and, every so often, surreptitiously took a look at my legs or my body. (Not surreptitiously enough—cougars are very observant, and I always managed to catch the glance.)

I bided my time and basked in his carefully camouflaged attention. I made sure to run into him whenever possible, and assumed that the opportunity to proceed to the next major step would present itself soon enough. I also thought he might engineer that opportunity himself. He did.

He invited me to a cocktail party. It was summertime and the evening was warm and pleasant. I dressed carefully. Sexy, sleeveless little black dress showing enough cleavage to be interesting but not sleazy. He had a rather prudish side that I found acutely intriguing—an obviously sexy and sensual man caught in the chains of inhibition. Grrr.

The dress was completed with a sharp, short white jacket and high-heeled sandals. To wear hose or not? I decided not, and then threw in my *piece de resistance*—no underwear. Not that anyone would ever know until the knowledge could be used to full advantage. Mine? His? We would see.

I arrived a little late (all the better to make an entrance) and didn't miss that he immediately saw me come through the door. I joined a group—not his, too blatant—and began to chat, eventually moving over to his group. I chatted with everyone. I made him laugh and ensured that I eventually ended up standing next to him. I touched his arm. Even though I knew he hated being touched, he didn't draw away.

The evening wore on and the wine soaked in. I was careful not to overindulge. I had plans that needed a clear head for good timing. People went home, leaving a very small group that included both of us. I talked about my next writing project—a piece on the sensuality of not wearing underwear. Those who didn't find the subject fascinating left. He stayed. When someone asked me whether I ever went without, I smiled a feline smile. Looking directly at him, I stated, "I'm not now." I watched with pleasure as his face flushed and he reached for his drink. We were on our way.

The group ended up as four—two women, two men—and I suggested relocating to another bar. Everyone agreed and we set off. The other bar was crowded, which was perfect. We had to crush together. Later, when he leaned in front of me to speak to someone else, I also leaned forward and quickly kissed his neck, just behind his ear. He forgot what he was saying and turned to me. "I think we should go back to my place," he said. I beamed at him, and walked toward the door holding his arm.

We went back to his place, seething with lust. As soon as the door was shut behind us, we kissed with an explosive passion that weakened both our knees—but not badly enough to prevent our trip to the bedroom. It was a fabulous night that I never wanted to end.

But I was a careful and clever cougar. Cougars never, ever give everything away during the first encounter. I made sure that he didn't see my entire repertoire and left enough mystery and titillation for him to want more. I was, I indicated, full of sexual secrets.

There was one small drawback. I had to leave on a plane at 7 a.m. the next morning. I spent the two-week trip in a high state of tumescence. So, apparently, did he. As soon as I returned, he was on the phone asking for another date. We got together that same night. It was the beginning of a full-blown, fiery affair.

The Confident Cougar

NO MATTER HOW strong, independent, and liberated a woman becomes, most (okay, all) are dissatisfied with at least one aspect of their appearance (okay, a lot of aspects …). This comes to a peak when she's looking for a new man. (If you've never changed outfits three times before a date, or jumped back into the shower to rewash your hair after a styling disaster, then skip the next two chapters—they were not written for the perfect.)

Cougars, however, are different from most women. Cougars know how to cope. Experienced cougars know that looking good helps you feel good, and that feeling good is vital when it comes to self-confidence—that magical quality that attracts men like a magnet. Cougars look, feel, think, and bed young. And, of course, they want to keep it that way.

Once upon a time, diamonds were a girl's best friend. In today's youth-oriented and highly competitive world, a far better investment is the phone number of the best cosmetic surgeon and anti-aging physician in town.

Forget the high-mindedness. Once considered a "vanity," cosmetic surgery is a now major growth industry. It's an acknowledged way to improve on nature, and a recognized path to increased self-confidence. And despite very exciting trends in anti-aging techniques, cosmetic surgery is still the only guaranteed way of maintaining that youthful look that cougars crave. It's also expensive and (sometimes) painful. But for cougars, it can be the kindest cut.

Cosmetic Surgery

IF YOU FEEL strongly that cosmetic surgery can help you look and feel your best, then it's right for you. Don't listen to anyone who says that you don't need it, or wonders aloud why you'd put yourself through such a thing. You're a cougar and you know what you want! Yup. Eternal youth.

The first step is to find a reputable surgeon that you like and with whom you feel comfortable. It's also vital that he or she understand exactly what you want to achieve. Your goals and needs must be realistic and achievable. Waving a photo of Gwyneth Paltrow under his nose and saying that you want to look just like her won't help or work.

One of the best ways to find a good surgeon is to talk to women who have had cosmetic surgery. This can be somewhat difficult if they want you to believe that they look fantastic because they a) have just returned from a long vacation, b) are working out more, c) are on a diet, or d) have just landed a hot young lover. If you draw a blank, call your local plastic surgery association and get the names of qualified surgeons in your area. Visit at least three before making your decision.

Be aware that all major cosmetic surgery has health risks, requires sedation or general anesthesia, and will need three to four weeks of recovery (and much longer for full healing).

Here are some of the newer techniques available from top surgeons today.

FACE AND NECK

Cougars may spend hours keeping their bodies toned, fit, and youthful. They certainly want their faces to match. These days,

Gwyneth envy

the upper two-thirds of the face can be rejuvenated and elevated endoscopically, eliminating the need for large incisions. Tiny telescopes are used to reposition droopy brows, cheeks, and mid-face areas, lift the corners of mouths, and eliminate smile lines. Even those dreaded jowls can get a partial pick-me-up with this method.

- Eyes: The contemporary approach to eye surgery is to preserve and reposition fat, avoiding the "hollowed out" look that was once so common. Lower lid surgery can now be done behind the eye and inside the lower lid. Fat bags are gone and the lower lid is left scarless.
- Nose: As women age, the tip of the nose tends to droop. A rhinoplasty will reposition it to look more youthful and balance the bridge.
- Lips: Full sensual lips are a definite sign of youth. Micro fat transplantation and the newer injectable fillers are being used to create fuller lips that look both younger and natural.
- Neck: Wrinkly necks can be smoothed by lifting and tightening the facial muscles (along with the loose skin) to give a longer-lasting and more effective lift.

BREASTS

Young men (okay, all men) are fascinated by women's breasts. Theories as to why abound, but they're not important. What is important is that a cougar is happy with hers—especially when it comes to wearing low-cut wardrobe choices.

Augmentation is still very popular and can now be carried out endoscopically (no scarring). Implants are filled with salt water or a cohesive gel that holds the shape of the breast. These days, women can also choose the shape—teardrop or round. Breast lifting (without implantation) can rejuvenate the breasts by removing excess skin and maintaining the same breast volume in a perkier position.

STOMACH

The traditional "tummy tuck" is still the method of choice for an aging stomach. It can remove loose skin, tighten loose muscles, and erase unattractive stretch marks. An endoscopic tummy tuck tightens and flattens an untoned, bulging stomach. Since no skin is removed during this procedure, healthy, non-damaged skin is a must.

BODY SCULPTING

While not a solution for those looking to lose a lot of weight, liposuction can be used to sculpt body contours. As a woman ages, unwanted body fat appears on the upper arms, neck, outer and inner thighs, hips, waist, abdomen, inner knees, and buttocks. (Is there anywhere it doesn't appear?) This fat can be removed by the insertion of a cannula—a metallic reed-like tube that draws out the fat. Micro cannulas help minimize trauma and injury. An anesthetic solution is often injected into the fat to plump it up before removal which minimizes bleeding and bruising. A new advancement involves the use of ultrasound energy. In this method, the sound waves liquefy the fat, making it easier to remove.

Artificial implants for cheeks are gaining popularity among those looking for a fuller, more youthful contour (also for buttocks for those who admire a more J. Lo look).

Non-Surgical Options

IF THE THOUGHT of "going under the knife" makes you pale, there are new, exciting, and amazing anti-aging alternatives breaking through in medicine. Scientists already know how to decipher the genetic code; they are also able to test the level of a person's DNA damage and then repair it. Analytical tests like these—tests that can lead to the repair of our aging cells—will mean that, eventually, it will be possible to manipulate a person's DNA to optimize his or her anti-aging abilities. People will live far longer—and far healthier—and not suffer the current debilitating damage that ages them. In an Orwellian sense, these new genetical and biomedical advances mean that the future of cosmetic surgery may well be no surgery at all—we just won't age! (A happy cougar thought.)

Anti-Aging Products and Supplements

These offer the least invasive way to look and feel good and combat aging from the inside out. One of the most popular methods of keeping aging (especially the effects of menopause) at bay is hormone therapy. Hormone therapy can help invigorate a slowing system and keep skin and hair youthful. It can also reduce menopausal symptoms such as hot flashes, irritability, and decreased vaginal lubrication—oh-so-important to the sex-loving cougar.

For those who prefer a more holistic approach, naturally occurring substances and nutraceuticals can also be taken to augment the body's natural release of hormones.

For the latest in non-invasive, anti-aging techniques, consult a physician who specializes in anti-aging medicine. For more information, search under "anti-aging" on the Internet. Two excellent sites are the Longevity Institute International and the American Academy of Anti-Aging Medicine (http://www.longevity-institute.com and http://www.worldhealth.net.a4m/html).

LASER, SKIN CARE, AND COSMETIC DERMATOLOGICAL SERVICES

No matter how much you exercise and eat right, the odd blemish will still crop up from time to time no matter what age you are (or appear to be …). Those that don't respond to surface creams and potions—such as spider veins, brown spots, large pores, and wrinkles—can be dealt with permanently by several methods.

♈ Photofacials and photorejuvenation. These are non-invasive, outpatient, laser- and intense pulsed-light techniques for lessening spider veins, rosacea, brown spots, and age spots.

They can also reduce pore size and smooth wrinkles. Photofacial therapy has no down time, no recovery time, and makeup can be applied immediately afterward. (Hurray!) A sort of medical takeout system for those on the run.

- ♈ Laser resurfacing techniques. Laser work is very popular, highly advanced, and acknowledged as the best answer to selectively remove layers of wrinkled and rough skin. This allows new skin to regenerate and grow. The actual process is fast, but recovery time is a minimum of two weeks.

- ♈ Laser hair removal. Extra fur may suit the real feline but city cougars prefer smooth skin. If you're tired of waxing, shaving, and plucking, superfluous hair can be removed by painless laser techniques. These are fast and affordable methods for upper lip, chin, sideburns, underarms, legs, and bikini line.

- ♈ Chemical peels. Peels use alpha or beta hydroxy acids or glycolic acid to remove several layers of skin via the application of chemical acids. A light peel will result in a few days of redness and flaking; deeper peels using Phenol or TCA (trichloroacetic acid) require two to three weeks of recovery.

- ¥ Microdermabrasion. This technique uses either tiny crystals or ultrasonic energy to basically scour away the skin's top surface, removing shallow wrinkles, lip lines, and small scars.
- ¥ Vein removal. The newest techniques are minimally invasive and use ultrasounds that diagnose where the deep veins are leaking—the cause of enlarged and varicose veins. Once these leaky veins are identified, tiny catheters are inserted to emit either a laser wavelength or a radio frequency to close off the leak. Once the large varicose veins have been closed, the superficial spider veins are removed with lasers or traditional sclerotherapy.
- ¥ Cellulite and stretch marks. Body wraps and endermologic techniques are mobilization and manipulation therapies that are successful in combating the dreaded "orange peel" look of skin, usually on the buttocks and thighs. Lasers and microdermabrasion are effective when applied to minimize stretch marks.

MEDICAL-GRADE SKIN CARE PRODUCTS

Anti-aging doctors now have an arsenal of active products to keep skin healthy, clear, and young. These physician-prescribed products have more potency than over-the-counter creams and lotions. Some of the newest and most effective are: derivatives of vitamin A (such as Retinol and Retin A); derivatives of vitamin C; Hydroquinone and Kogic acid to lighten and brighten skin; Co-enzyme Q10 L acid lotions to diminish skin damage and promote collagen production. These products can have untoward side effects and should be taken only after consultation with your doctor.

NON-SURGICAL FACE LIFTING

Yes, it is possible to get good, youthful-looking results without surgery. There are, in fact, several non-invasive methods available. Injectable fillers—such as collagen or the newer hyaluronic acids (Restylane, Perlane, and Hylaform)—are used to smooth wrinkles and lines; they also cause fewer allergic reactions than collagen. The beneficial effects of these products last about three months.

Longer-lasting injectable filling products (one to two years) are Artecoll and your own fat—drawn from areas of your body where there is excess (Choices! Choices!). There are also implantable substances, such as Gortex, that can provide long-term filling of wrinkles and furrows.

Injectable paralytics such as Botox and Monobloc put the facial muscles to sleep to get rid of frown lines, crow's feet, forehead lines, and neck bands and cords. The results last about four months.

New electrical stimulation techniques can isotonically contract and exercise the muscles of your face to elevate brows, cheeks, and neck.

Y

All the information above is intentionally brief. It is offered only as a guideline to some of the current advances in anti-aging and rejuvenation. Professional doctors, cosmetic plastic surgeons, and anti-aging specialists should always be consulted.

Cosmetic surgery and anti-aging consultant: Dr. R. Stephen Mulholland, M.D., SpaMedica Cosmetic Surgery and Infinite Vitality Clinic, Toronto, Ontario, Canada.

The Bare Facts

SO COUGARS ARE stylish, confident women who know what they want and know how to get it, right? Right. But no matter how sexy, sleek, and just plain gorgeous she looks with her clothes on, even the most confident cougar can get a little squeamish when it comes to removing her clothes. Hitherto unfaced fears—"has my body aged badly?", "is my cellulite/stretch mark/extra weight showing?", "what happens when I take off my push-up bra?"—rear their ugly heads and can put a real damper on a promising evening.

Hopefully, you'll at least have clean underwear on. If it's reasonably sexy, you're ahead of the game. But if all this happens to be a spontaneous event and you've still got on the plain Jane stretch cottons you wore yesterday, try not to worry. If you've done good cougar work, he'll be so hot to trot that he won't even give them a glance.

A couple of cautionary notes on bedding younger prey. Since at some point you will wonder if you're competing for a medal in the sexual Olympics, it helps considerably to be flexible and fit. A muscle cramp in the middle of an accelerating orgasmic experience is humiliating, not to mention painful. You can try gritting your teeth and practicing pain management techniques but cramps generally call an immediate halt to the proceedings and disappoint everyone, including yourself. While doing a series of stretch exercises before clambering into bed might actually be fascinating for a young man to watch (especially if you do them in the nude), it is far better to ensure you're up to the job, so to speak. Get fit and flexible.

This Magic Moment

EVEN IF YOU'RE a calm, confident cougar with plenty of martinis under your belt, and even if your young prey is lolling about with his tongue hanging out, there's still a moment or two of discomfiture. The younger man may be wondering if this is a

Good Idea after All. If he's very young, he may be thinking about what his mother would say if she knew where he was.

Before you can turn around after lighting the candles, your young man will have all of his clothes off and scattered about the room. Younger men undress at lightning speed when sex is on the horizon; and while it's obviously desirable to shower first, a hot cougar's need to get to the nitty gritty as fast as possible can cancel plans for a sniff test.

The glorious sight of your quarry laying naked on the bed will probably speed up your disrobing as well. If you're still worried about figure flaws, cellulite, and stretch marks, simply undress with your back to the bed. When you swing around stark naked, he will succumb to stimulating impact that female nakedness always has on members of his species.

If you can resist the urge to pounce, start the proceedings by massaging him with your best essential oils. Lay him on his stomach, ignoring all complaints about discomfort to a certain all-too-ready part and whines of "but I thought were going to. . . ." Now's the time to teach him that a skilled cougar delivers—in her own time. Explain that the major pleasure of arriving at any destination is the journey itself. If he gives you trouble, sit firmly on his backside.

Separating the Cougars from the Pumas

STILL WORRIED ABOUT your figure faults? Take a tip from the strategy of war. When he turns over, attack and surprise, diving down on him with your mouth. (Tip: Decide the essential matter of condom application well beforehand.) The delight and surprise will make him close his eyes for a moment, providing you with the perfect opportunity to lower yourself while still orally attached. (Tip: Watch your teeth. Nothing deflates a moment more than the crunch of molars.)

Skilled oral sex is, by the way, what separates the cougars from the pumas. Pumas tend to think that oral sex is something to be done quickly and repetitively, like devouring a melting ice cream cone. Cougars know better. They're aware that what they have in their mouths is a complex system of nerve endings and sensitivity which, if handled skillfully and artfully, will ensure the complete and ongoing devotion of the captured prey. The cougar also knows that if matters are accelerating too fast, she can use the effective ten-second pressure technique to slow things down. Good cougars know what this is, and where and how to do it.

With luck, your oral sex skills will encourage him to reciprocate. This willing sexual sharing is one of the great pleasures of landing younger prey. (Many older men still think oral sex is only for them.) What's more, you'll likely discover that he's quite skilled! With older men, you might have found yourself thinking about the new sofa you wanted to buy and wondering whether or not you should change the carpet at the same time. With your younger man, it will be "no, no, I can't manage another orgasm." But you will.

Positions of Power

BY THIS TIME, the action will be pretty hot and heavy, and your prey may be doing a fine rendition of a volcano about to erupt. If figure faults are still in your mind (and I'd be very surprised if they were), it's time to wrap your arms around him, kiss him passionately, and get into what used to be known as the Missionary Position. Yes, I know why it's called that, but I prefer to interpret it as "ready to go anywhere," which is how you should be feeling right now. (He certainly is.)

There's only one small problem. Lying on your back is not the best way to display your most precious assets—your breasts. If you've had implants, than you don't need to worry—your breasts will stand up like the nose cones on space rockets no matter which way you lie. But if they've lost their perk and tend to slide like a pair of fried eggs into your armpits, just keep your arms tight to your body. Instant fullness. (Tip: I've found that squeezing your arms extra tight into your sides at precisely the right moment can give up an extra boost, accelerating the young man's reaction if he's lying flat on top of you. Handy if he's very heavy and you're about to asphyxiate.)

If this is obviously going to be a long session (remember what I said about stamina), this may be an ideal moment to change positions. Many young men like to be behind their partners during sex. Not only can they don any ridiculous facial expression they want, they also get an unobstructed view of their own part and yours—in all its exposed glory. Since time does not ravage such areas, cougars consider this position particularly beneficial. There are other perks, as well. Your backside will look remarkably firm and round and your waist will positively shrink. Breasts and full frontal nudity may be the stuff that Hollywood is made of, but wise cougars know that backs and bums are much prettier—and stay firmer longer.

At some point, you will undoubtedly move into the position that dominates most male fantasies—on top. This can present a bit of a challenge. As erotic as this position might be for them, it also allows gravity to kick in for you. Everything falls forward—face, chin, breasts, and stomach. This doesn't necessarily mean that you're stuck with the Missionary Position for the rest of your life. Smart cougars have a tactic that sidesteps full exposure in this position—head down, bum up.

Getting on top takes skill. Rapid impaling is not only foolish but can be damaging to all concerned. Many a painful bend has occurred when an over-enthusiastic cougar has pounced with too much speed and enthusiasm. Far better to slide into position. Move your head into the side of his neck and slowly slide backwards into the crouch position, making sure to keep your bum raised. Once this has been achieved, you may find it necessity to sit up at some point—probably because you have a cramp in your knees or thighs or can't breathe. And yes, all will be exposed at that moment. But, believe me: by this time, your prey will be happily treading the path to sexual heaven. He simply will not notice or care whether you have a stretch mark here or sag there. Besides, from his position—lying down, looking up—there is no such thing as droop. (Although I do admit that I once got into this position on my own and put a large hand mirror on the pillow to check things out. Quite frankly, it put me off the on top position for a while.)

Feeling experimental? Try a variation on the theme. Whip around and mount him the other way—so that he's looking at your well-toned back. Again, caution is recommended regarding speed. Nature intended for certain male pieces of equipment to fit certain female pieces at a certain angle. The position that you're currently in doesn't even come close. As a result, it will also take considerable concentration to get the movement right—an odd combination of simultaneous backwards, forwards, and downwards sliding. Yes, it takes practice, but practicing on young men is indeed perfect.

This position has a lot of merit. It not only hides your figure faults, it can slim your thighs if you do it frequently enough. (I lost a whole inch one summer with a willing young teacher.) If you sense a heavy case of the fatigues coming on and need to bring matters to a close, this position has the power to do just that. Increase the speed of your movement and exhilaration is imminent.

Post Pounce

IT'S WISE TO know that a climax for a younger man is not the same as for an older man. Older men will climax and then collapse in a snoring heap or want a beer. Younger men will want more action. This may require more energy and effort than the average cougar has time to expend on the delights of sex. Besides, you're probably fighting the urge to collapse in a snoring heap yourself.

Try to encourage time to lie together and delightedly post-mortem the activities over a chilled glass of wine. This will only work if your mascara hasn't smudged to the point where it's making you look like a raccoon. If this has, in fact, happened, slide into your best silky robe (your comfy house grubby will not do) and visit the bathroom for repairs and a spritz of fragrance. You can then reappear as a sleek sophisticated predator—a transformation your prey will find worldly and quite irresistible (if he hasn't collapsed in a snoring heap.)

Perhaps the evening has ended up as an overnighter, which means that the bright light of dawn might not be far away. For cougars, as for Count Dracula, this can be a fearful and unflattering time. She has, after all, spent the entire night bouncing enthusiastically under and over the sheets. If you feel that without makeup you look as though death is imminent, slip quietly away while he sleeps and fix things up. You don't want him calling an ambulance when he opens his eyes.

Nowadays, though, most cougars prefer the techie idea of WYSIWYG—what you see is what you get. In any case, the point is probably moot. A good cougar will have her prey so mesmerized that she could look like the Bride of Frankenstein. It won't matter. He'll still wake up ready to go again.

Sometimes, it's wise to land the prey, bed him, and then send him home. Many illusions (not to mention restful nights of sleep) have been preserved by ending the evening before the candles have burned down or the sun has come up. He'll leave wanting a return engagement and you'll still be totally in control. The only parting line for any cougar worth her whiskers? "Thank you, that was great. Don't call me, I'll call you."

The Fine Print

ALL COUGARS SHOULD be aware of the necessity for carrying—and, more importantly, using—condoms. No matter how carried away on the wild tide of lust and desire you are (and I know only too well how giddy and immune to reality that can make anyone feel), it's downright dangerous to have sex without protection.

"Don't call me…"

It's often difficult for a cougar to maintain this discipline. She hails from an era when sexually transmitted diseases weren't widespread and trust was respected. The male of yesteryear hated condoms (many still do). In order to convince women to take pity on them and go without, they said that wearing a condom during sex was like taking a bath in an overcoat. Eager to please the male species, many women were easily persuaded.

In those days all sexually transmitted diseases were generally lumped together under the heading VD (venereal diseases), and most women knew relatively little about them. We were taught that Henry VIII had VD and probably gave it to all his wives, whom he then undoubtedly blamed (which might explain the constant beheading). Prostitutes spread it— although none of us had ever seen one, met one, or knew anyone who had gone to one. Nice Ladies were never supposed to have heard of it, let alone get it. Although sex was always a hot topic, disease was never discussed in polite society. And besides, none of us had sex until we were engaged or married in those days. The only way to learn anything about sexually transmitted diseases was to surreptitiously slide one of those pamphlets available at doctors' offices into your bag during your visit. You had to search for them, though, as anything of that nature was well hidden in case it offended anyone.

Today, if it looks as if she's going to land her prey and get him where she wants him—between the sheets or wherever—a smart cougar will ask outright about HIV tests, use her own condoms if possible, and still check him out. He, being younger and more comfortable with this sexual minefield, will also check her out. Cougars are always prepared.

Cougars are well-informed and constantly aware of the risks of having multiple partners. These risks have gradually turned society back around to embracing what's been called the New Monogamy. To a cougar, this means just one at a time.

Attacks

WHILE YOU AND your young prey are happily snuggled—or otherwise occupied—under the sheets, it's easy to forget the world outside. Unfortunately, it's not likely that the outside world will forget about you. Although the world in general doesn't give a fig nowadays about what people do (as long as it doesn't interfere with their lives or raise prices), when it comes to older women dating younger men society's reaction is not always positive.

The more traditional older man / younger women relationship is easily accepted, mainly because men have insisted on it for centuries. (What better way to flaunt their sexual dominance?) They simply take the tack that dating a twenty-four year old is perfectly natural. Which is, of course, what cougars should say about their activities.

But despite all the strides made in sexual attitudes, the world still has problems accepting an older woman/younger man pairing. It's the old double standard—especially since both partnerships are essentially built on the same needs and desires. Just like older men, cougars want to feel young. They want someone on their arm who is youthful, optimistic, and stimulating. They also want hot, steamy sex with someone who looks good—both in and out of his clothes. The main differences? Cougars aren't trying to prove their virility, hook someone by getting pregnant, or land a long-term relationship. Cougars prefer the short and sweet approach.

It's not too difficult to see that the most hostile reaction to a cougar's activities will come from older men. For years, they have been secure in the knowledge that they are the ones that choose and discard partners at will, especially as these partners age. Now, cougars are treading on their territory, making them feel threatened and insecure. With the tables turned, older *men* are finding themselves discarded for younger ones. The message is clear. Cougars don't want older men because they are too old. It's enough to turn their hair even whiter under the Grecian Formula.

But older men aren't the only ones with axes to grind. Older women (the ones who aren't cougars themselves, that is) find themselves torn between social indoctrination and restrictions, envy, and jealousy. Whatever their jumble of feelings, they'll be critical and condemning while secretly wishing they were in your place. Ex-husbands and lovers (yours and his), your girlfriends and their mates, his friends, and even the service industry will all have a choice word or two.

So as you can see, all the world does not love a lover—especially when she's with a younger man.

The Separated or Divorced Older Man

THEY ARE A MAJOR source of hostility when it comes to older women dating younger men, for all the reasons listed above. You're on their territory, they feel threatened and insecure, and you're making them feel old. This is all much worsened if they (a) have just gone through their separation/divorce; (b) haven't found another partner yet; (c) are going through midlife crisis, or; (d) are suffering from impotence (or erectile dysfunction, as it's know these days). Of course, this last reason just might be why you're now a cougar!

What He'll Ask if You're on Your Own

- Y Is he your son?
- Y What do you talk about with such a big generation gap?
- Y Don't you feel foolish dating boys?
- Y Are you on hormone replacement therapy yet?
- Y Is he old enough to drink?
- Y Want a date with a Real Man?
- Y How much do escorts cost these days?

What He'll Do if You're With Your Date

- Y Ignore him completely and talk only to you.
- Y Talk incessantly about his money/expensive car/electronic toys/boat/new condo/cottage/stocks.
- Y Be too friendly, giving you hugs and kisses even though you hardly know him.
- Y Introduce his own date and give her age, which will probably be under thirty (checkmate him by saying that your date is two years younger).
- Y Talk about how many times he has sex in one night.
- Y Ask your date when you're getting married.

If he persists, ignore all of his barbs and look very happy, relaxed, and satisfied. This isn't difficult when dating younger men. If you're really under pressure, ask him if it isn't time he took his medication.

COPING

Not all men in this category are unpleasant and antagonistic. Some are supportive and full of admiration for your chutzpah. But if you feel even a small wave of resentment coming from them don't get into conversation about aging, sex, or dating younger men. Avoid talking about impotence or prostate cancer like the plague.

Wait a minute—you're a cougar! Let him have it!

Your Ex

YOUR EX'S REACTION to the news that you're now dating someone twenty or more years younger than him will, of course, depend on why you broke up, how bitter or friendly it was, and how your relationship with him is at present. Actually, no matter what happened when you split, he'll be difficult.

What He'll Say

- ♈ The young man is after your money (if you got a good settlement).
- ♈ You must be going through a midlife crisis (if you didn't get a good settlement ... not a smart cougar!).
- ♈ You always were a slut and were lousy in bed.
- ♈ The young man has a mother complex.
- ♈ The young man is a gigolo, or that he's an addict/alcoholic/homeless/gay.
- ♈ You "went to pieces" after your split and are doing this out of spite.

What He'll Do

- ♈ Rush out and buy the latest hot car (something sporty and expensive), install a hot young thing in the passenger seat, and drive by your house (just to show you he's still top dog).
- ♈ Hire a top lawyer (if you haven't yet divorced) to make sure the young man doesn't get a dime.
- ♈ Become very social, have parties in your old house, and make sure you hear about them.
- ♈ Consider cosmetic surgery, even though he sneered when you had yours.

🍸 Want more access (or less) with the kids and tell them you've "gone wacky."

🍸 Question the kids closely about what you do and where you go.

If he says or does none of the above and greets the young man warmly with hugs, watch out. He could be redefining his sexuality. No matter how amicable your relationship is, you will tell your young man that your ex was alcoholic/impotent/unfaithful/abusive and lousy in bed.

COPING

Keep a low profile until your ex's anger and bitterness has subsided (if it ever does). Don't take your young man to friends' houses or parties for a while and don't go to the places where you always went with your ex. Start a new pattern.

Wait a minute—you're a cougar! Flaunt him!

His Ex

IN MY EXPERIENCE, young women have a huge hissy fit when they find out they've been dumped for an older woman. His ex-wife or girlfriend will react in much the same way as your ex-husband when she discovers that her former mate has fallen prey to a cougar.

What She'll Say

- Y He has a mother complex.
- Y You're a slut/child abuser/nymphomaniac/alcoholic/whore.
- Y You've had implants and massive cosmetic surgery.
- Y You've lied about your age and are, in fact, much older.
- Y He's definitely after your money (as he's already spent all of hers).

What She'll Do

- Y Hire a top lawyer (if they haven't divorced yet) to make sure she gets far more than she deserves.
- Y Immediately hook up with a handsome younger man in order to demonstrate how desirable she is.
- Y Manipulate his access time with the kids and tell them you're a Blair Witch.
- Y Pack up all his old junk, accidentally including their honeymoon photos.
- Y Have dinner with your ex to find out more about you.

If she says or does none of the above and greets you with warm hugs, watch out. She was probably glad to get rid of him and is shocked that anyone would want him. No matter how nice she was, your younger man will say that his ex was alcoholic/ frigid/unfaithful/abusive/a nag and lousy in bed.

COPING

Try not to mention his ex. If you must, make sure to never criticize her or his children. Advise him to treat her honorably and make sure you don't meet anywhere. Don't try to influence any of her friends.

Wait a minute—you're a cougar! Go ahead!

Your Girlfriends

YOUR GIRLFRIENDS WILL fall into two categories—those who are cougars themselves and those who aren't but wish they were. The former will think your new relationship is great fun. The latter will think it's foolish. Both will want to know everything in great detail—especially about the sex.

Your Cougar Friends Will ...

- ⟁ Ask how old he is, and smile when you answer.
- ⟁ Make you the star guest at their parties, dinners, and barbecues.
- ⟁ Congratulate you and say that they envy your freedom from marital ties.
- ⟁ Start going to the gym more often, visit a spa, and get a complete makeover.
- ⟁ Ask you whether their teenage son is attractive.

Your Non-Cougar Friends Will ...

- ⟁ Tell you he's after your money.
- ⟁ Ask if he's your son's friend.
- ⟁ Invite you over only to introduce you to their male older single friends.
- ⟁ Remind you of your age, tell you how successful and wealthy their husbands are, and wax poetic about how nice it is to be secure.
- ⟁ Tell you they're "aging gracefully," wear "suitable" clothes, and let their hair go gray to show you what "reality" looks like.

- ✲ Ask if you're drinking too much.
- ✲ Go out with you more—without him.
- ✲ Talk about all the gross things you've done together in front of him.
- ✲ Discuss at length anything they feel sure he knows nothing about, especially if he wasn't born when it happened.
- ✲ Get nervous when you start chatting to their sons.

Both groups will tell you about the younger men that have approached them. Your cougar friends will hint that they, too, have enjoyed such liaisons. The others will say that they turned them down. Both will say your relationship won't last.

COPING

As for your cougar friends, enjoy their camaraderie. Just make sure your younger man isn't left too long alone with them. ...

Wait a minute—you're a cougar! Show your girlfriends what they're missing!

No need to do much about your non-cougar friends because you'll look so happy, fit, and glowing and be wearing such a satisfied smile, they'll soon retreat into silence.

Your Girlfriends' Partners

USUALLY IN THE older men category, your friends' husbands and boyfriends will not take your new relationship well. They're afraid their wives or girlfriends will want to do the same. (Never mind that they may have had the occasional dalliance with a young woman outside their partnership. They probably believe they're entitled and that it's different for women.)

WHAT THEY'LL SAY
- You're doing it just to spite your ex.
- He's after your money.
- He's looking for a mother.
- You're going through a midlife crisis and/or menopause.

WHAT THEY'LL DO
- Resent you because their partners have already started nagging them about their weight/smoking/drinking/gray hair.
- Discourage their partners from visiting you, especially if your boyfriend's around.
- Ask your young man what he does and mention the millions *they* made last year in stock options.

🍸 Ask how your ex is doing, in front of your new man.

🍸 Have a temper tantrum if the young man beats them at chess or Trivial Pursuit.

COPING

Remember that, in the end, girlfriends are worth their weight in gold. Stick it out with their partners' barbs. Warn your young man ahead of time when you're visiting them, and let your girlfriends cope with their partners' petulance and insecurity. After all, they're probably experts at it by now.

Wait a minute—you're a cougar! Show your claws! Ask them if their Viagra tablets are working yet....

His Friends

A VERY GOOD measure of a young man's maturity is how he deals with the curiosity, questions, and outright barbs of his closest friends. Chances are good that they'll think he's lost his marbles—unless you look like Julia Roberts or are very rich and famous, in which case you'll be overwhelmed with their gushing approval. Their wives/girlfriends will tear you to pieces behind your back.

What They'll Say

- ♟ He's been hit in the head with a puck.
- ♟ He's on drugs.
- ♟ He should "go for it" (your money, that is).
- ♟ It won't last.

What They'll Do

- ♟ Keep telling him what he's missing (namely "young" and "gorgeous").
- ♟ Hint that dating you could wreck his career.
- ♟ Lay bets on how old you are.
- ♟ Ask if you're his mother's friend.
- ♟ Arrange blind dates for him with young women, *any* young women.
- ♟ Go out with him more—without you.
- ♟ Talk about the gross things they've done together in front of you.
- ♟ Discuss at length anything they feel sure you know nothing about (which is almost everything they do).

Strangely, because their girlfriends are so against you, his male friends just might embrace you with youthful enthusiasm.

Male bonding being the weird and unfathomable ritual that it is, if you aren't in with their women, you must be okay.

COPING

If pressure from his friends wrecks your relationship, be thankful. He's obviously not ready or mature enough for the bold, sophisticated world of the cougar. He is, in other words, poor prey.

Wait a minute—you're a cougar! You didn't want him to stick around anyway!

Your Families

NEVER, EVER IGNORE the influence of family pressure on your new relationship. It can be immense, emotional, unrelenting, and devious—especially where mothers are concerned. Why the dinosaur thinking? Let's not forget the ancient concept that still lingers in the dark caves of many minds: relationships are formed in order to procreate the species. For the mother— yours or his—eagerly awaiting the promotion to "grandmother," older women dating younger men are a threat to this "natural" human progression.

HIS FAMILY WILL ...
- Panic and call your relationship a family crisis.
- Say he's just getting sexual "experience."
- Say he's after your money.
- Continuously invite "suitable" girls to family events.
- Talk incessantly about the future—when he'll be married and have kids.
- Say he's making his mother ill.
- Bribe him to stop seeing you (try and get them to bribe you instead).

YOUR FAMILY WILL ...
- Worry what the neighbors think.
- Say that you were always oversexed.
- Remind you constantly about your age.
- Ask if you're going through menopause.
- Say you're making your mother ill.
- Tell you you're making a fool of yourself.
- Say he's after your money.

COPING

Keep home visits with your younger man to a minimum, especially to his family. For a blameless and unassailable excuse, plead "a business commitment." Although both families might think you're a workaholic, his will probably hope you're making tons of money so they can boast about you.

Wait a minute—you're a cougar! When visiting *his* family, turn up looking confidant and fabulous (not difficult for a cougar). When visiting yours, beam happily and say that looking young and dating younger men must be in your genes.

The Maître D'

NOWADAYS PEOPLE HARDLY notice whether couples are old/young, same sex, or whatever. The one place that this does not hold true is in a quality restaurant. While most people will ignore you when you're out with your young man, you'll find that the service industries will undoubtedly ask you first for your order and expect you to make the payment. Don't be surprised if you get the lousy table normally reserved for women on their own. At functions, you will be subject to a mixture of curiosity, envy, resentment, jealousy, and disapproval. This will

The Maitre D' in love

ease slightly if your date is incredibly handsome or if you look so young that you appear to be close in age.

What He'll Do

- ♈ Look your date up and down with disdain.
- ♈ Direct all conversation to you.
- ♈ Lustfully eye your date.
- ♈ Give you the wine list.
- ♈ Pour the sample into your glass, even if your date ordered.
- ♈ Present you with the check.

Coping

It's a good idea to settle the issue of payment before heading out. Once at the restaurant, don't hesitate to ask for a different table if you don't like the one offered. If your young man ordered the wine, tell the waiter he must taste the sample first. And, above all, make sure the waiter knows that your date is straight.

Wait a minute—you're a cougar! Stay home and eat takeout in bed!

Finally, it's worth noting that not everyone reacts badly. When I told my late mother that I was dating a very special man who was much younger than me, she asked me his age. I told her. After a pause, she cheerfully said, "Nice age, dear!"

It was.

The Tender Trap

ON THE WHOLE, a cougar could care less what anyone thinks or says about her various conquests. She hunts to satisfy her own needs, not the outdated expectations of society at large. This laissez-faire attitude is an essential part of being a cougar. It's part of her confidence, her allure, and her ability to stay true to herself. It's also much easier to maintain if she's on the hunt for short-term pleasure.

Many cougars become cougars because they're not into long-term commitment. Today's cougar knows that less is definitely more. She wants short-term pleasure, companionship, and frequent sex. She's come to this realization after many years of living on other people's terms. Now, in the prime of her life, she's focused on her own wants and needs. Long-term commitments take more time, energy, and attention than she's willing to give.

Why Less is More

- ♈ A cougar may have an expanding career, with little time left over for recreation. She wants to be left alone to spend her time as she sees fit.
- ♈ A cougar may have already had one or more marriages or several long-term live-in relationships. She's tired of being a servant or of giving so much for so little.
- ♈ A cougar may be intensely private. She doesn't want to share her personal space—especially her closet.
- ♈ A cougar may like being single. She feels no need to be a "smug-married."
- ♈ A cougar may want to fulfill her sexual needs when and where she wants to. She doesn't want to feel obligated to call the next day.
- ♈ A cougar may want total control over her life. She doesn't want to have to consider anyone else's opinions, wants, or needs.

Best intentions aside, the control issue is a feminine impossibility when it comes to matters of the heart. Let's face it, it's difficult for even a hunt-hardened cougar not to occasionally fall

into the Tender Trap. On rare occasions, a cougar will find herself in love. It's a natural situation, and while it's quite possible
for the relationship to end in co-habitation or even marriage, it's
much more likely that it will end up broken—just like most
other relationships today.

If you do decide to pursue a long-term relationship, do so with
eyes wide open. Enjoy it while it lasts, but know that it probably
won't last for long—and it definitely won't last forever. There are
many reasons why your relationship might break up: money differences; career demands and changes; social, peer, and family pressures; affairs; disagreements about having a family; the inability to
do so; changing goals in life; loss of desire; selfishness; jealousy;
growing apart; and immaturity. The list is practically endless—and
is identical to the list of factors that can end any other relationship.

Contrary to popular belief, your older woman/younger man
relationship will rarely break up just because you're getting old.
Nor will your man inevitably dump you for a younger woman.
It's worth remembering that your age was part of what attracted
him in the first place, and that the dreaded generation gap nar-
rows as the years pass. And besides, it can be the other way
around. You may dump him for another younger man.

Nevertheless, if you are committed to making your latest conquest stand the test of time, be aware of the land mines that lay in your path. What follows is a list of the most common. Approach with caution.

Procreation Panic

SAY THE WORD "baby" and most cougars will pale and reach for a double martini. Getting pregnant and having kids simply isn't part of the steamy world of hunter and prey.

This isn't to say that cougars don't think babies are cute and adorable. They do—as long as they belong to someone else and are kept far away from their designer clothes. But as cute and adorable as babies may be, cougars don't want them.

WHY COUGARS DON'T WANT BABIES

- She may already have one (or several) keeping her busy.
- She may be residing in an empty nest—and loving every minute of it.
- She may have a developing career that would suffer because of the demands of motherhood.
- She may enjoy her busy, fulfilling, child-free life.

- ♈ She may be heading into, going through, or finished with menopause.
- ♈ She may have some fancy knots tied internally.
- ♈ She'd have to give up smoking, drinking, and wild sex. (Perish the thought!)

Despite the fact that the "no baby" decision is often mutually agreeable at the outset of a older woman/younger man relationship, babies remain a major break-up factor once the relationship has become long-term and exclusive. It's the unfortunate result of falling in love and wanting to plan a future together—scary vocabulary for hardline cougars.

If hunter and prey do decide to make it a mating, the subject of babies must be dealt with right away. Why? Because one bright day in the not so distant future, your young man will succumb to Procreation Panic. Like most women his age, he realizes the clock is ticking. Never mind that he has the ability to create babies until the day he croaks (even if he's lost every other ability), he'll suddenly decide that he wants to be a father while he's still young enough to enjoy the experience. If you're unable or unwilling to comply, and won't consider adoption, you may have to face the harsh reality of him leaving to procreate with someone else—namely a puma. This is crunch time: a true test of whether his need to procreate is stronger than his need for the relationship, a true test of whether you can let go.

All of this does not mean that older women with younger partners never have babies. Many do—sometimes to satisfy their partner's needs, sometimes to satisfy their own. After all, young fathers have a lot going for them.

YOUNG FATHERS ARE ...

- more active than you
- likely to live longer than you
- closer in age to the child than you
- willing to share the responsibilities and problems of rearing a child. (They'll never say "it's a mother's job" when the little bundle screams in the middle of the night)
- willing to stay at home if you are not
- willing to be a loving father in public
- willing to be seen with baby spit on their sweater
- willing to change diapers and feed the baby without complaining or throwing up

In the end, the baby issue is a matter of choice—your choice. If it's not what you want, be upfront about your goals in life. It helps to discuss the matter fully when the relationship first gets serious—say, in the first week. The other answer is, of course, to follow that all-important, unspoken cougar rule: never, ever, get serious.

Children

CHILDREN ARE ONE OF the most likely factors to break up a cougar's relationship. For a start, kids usually resent their mother's finding someone else. (The strength of this resentment is directly related to how attached they are to their father.) The new relationship also raises the ugly thought of Parents Having Sex—only slightly less disgusting than the thought of stepping in dog poop. Depending on their age, most kids prefer to think their parents only did It once—in order to bring them into the world—and now that they've split, will remain celibate for the rest of their lives. It comes as a shock when their devoted mother begins to date. Suddenly, the possibility of Grown-Up Sex rears its ugly head.

Age is a crucial factor. If your kids are very young, they'll merely see your partner as another male adult friend. If they're older, they'll either be resentful or just plain curious—don't be surprised if they ask what kind of car he drives. If they're the same age, they'll be a nightmare.

Your Young Children Will ...

- Y want more attention than ever
- Y want to go everywhere with both of you
- Y want to play with him just when you want to (different games, of course)
- Y have tantrums when you hire a babysitter
- Y suddenly develop a stomachache/earache/fever/diarrhea just as you're about to go out
- Y want to share the bed when he stays over night (and then wet it)
- Y come into the room in the morning and stand at the bottom of the bed sobbing
- Y call him "Daddy" (which he'll hate)

YOUR OLDER CHILDREN WILL ...

- Y introduce him to their most attractive girlfriends (even if he only says "hi," they'll tell you he prefers younger women)
- Y insist on having more "family time"
- Y abandon the house altogether
- Y demand more money from you or want to use your car or cell phone all the time (they're counting on a little bit of guilt to help them out)
- Y report gossip about your young man's past
- Y make up gossip about your young man's past
- Y leave books like *Aging Gracefully*, *Mastering Menopause*, and *Kids are Very Important* lying on the coffee table
- Y talk about how fabulous, creative, and successful their father is (even if he's in jail)
- Y call their father and tell him what you're doing, over-embellishing the facts
- Y tell the rest of the family that you're "making a fool of yourself" and suggest that he's after your money

Your daughter might like him a little too much and flaunt herself in front of him; your son may refuse to stay in the same room. If your young man is rich, famous, or a sports star, they'll both adore him. If they're much older, with children of their own, they'll make sure the young man gets to meet the baby. They'll have taught it "gramma" as its first word—just to remind you of your age. They'll say you're going through a midlife crisis or menopause. Your family therapy bills may skyrocket.

His Children Will ...

- ♼ burst into tears every time you speak to them
- ♼ tell their mother that you didn't feed them (while refusing to eat anything you prepare)
- ♼ tell their father that you abuse them
- ♼ refuse to leave his side
- ♼ wreck your furniture and get candy stuck in the cat's fur
- ♼ want to join you in bed if they're staying overnight
- ♼ listen in on your conversations and repeat everything to their mother

Dealing with the baggage that children bring may be more than you want to handle. If this is the case, you should make it a rule to never date men with children. (In this day and age, though, that can be easier said than done.) Failing that, you can try to be sensitive to their needs and ease them into your new relationship. Let him handle his access time on his own. If his kids do turn up during your time together, never slip tranquilizers into their drinks (unless truly desperate). As for your kids, try meeting your young man outside the home until they get used to the idea of him, and don't plan overnight visits (not a problem for most cougars). Tell them that you love them, and then tell them that you're entitled to a life of your own. If all else fails, buy them lots of stuff.

Pumas

JUST IN CASE you weren't paying attention before, I'll say it again. Most people assume the major cause of a breakup between an older woman and a younger man will be a younger woman. This simply isn't true. People persist in believing this only because it vindicates their belief that the liaison is "against nature." They fail to understand a very simple fact—the younger man is dating the older woman because he likes and desires older women.

He's probably jaded by the demands of contemporary young pumas. He may feel that his encounters with them were more akin to job interviews than to dates. He may be sick of the Initial Interrogation. (What do you drive? Where do you work? Where do you live? How much do you earn? What'll you give me?) He may be fed up with the fancy footwork required to avoid talk of marriage, meeting parents, moving in, or kids—all on the second date.

A cougar offers a refreshing change. She's glamorous, stylish, and sexy. She's not demanding, whiny, or boring. As an added bonus, she has exactly the same interests in life as he does— laughing, drinking, playing, and making love. Irresistible to a young man.

If you are following the golden "short-term" rule, pumas don't even need to cross your mind. If, however, the relationship does become snared in the trap of love and togetherness, pumas can be a source of worry. What's worse, they can undermine your natural confidence.

It's true that most pumas see any young man who isn't married (and even some who are) as fair game. A man in a relationship with an older woman may be considered particularly easy meat. After all, young women are incessantly told by the entire world that they are the most desirable creatures on earth, and that getting older is some kind of slippery abyss into which women disappear. A smart cougar can survive the onslaught by observing a few pertinent rules of conduct.

SURVIVING A PUMA ATTACK

- ⅄ When passing a very attractive puma in the street, don't grab your partner's arm and point to something in the opposite direction. (He'll notice her anyway).
- ⅄ At parties, do not hang onto your date constantly, or rush across the room when you see him chatting to a young woman. (Unless she has big breasts and a low-cut dress.)
- ⅄ At social functions, mingle with the other guests, although finding the most attractive older man in the room to chat up is childish (even though it often works).
- ⅄ Do not constantly grill your partner about his puma colleagues. It's far better to believe they're all ugly and married (even if they look like Catherine Zeta-Jones).
- ⅄ Never go to company functions to check out pumas. (Well, only once or twice.)

137

♈ Do not insist on accompanying your mate everywhere, or ask him where he was if he's late. Prey should be let out of the cage occasionally or they'll turn on you.

Gorgeous younger women are everywhere, with more coming along all the time. It's a waste of time, effort, and emotion to be insecure. A true cougar will remember that the reason her young man is with her is because she's a fascinating, stylish, confidant, independent, sexually skilled older woman. Cougar Mantra: I'm fabulous, absolutely fabulous!

Other Young Men

THE TROUBLE WITH young men is that they're addictive. It's a fun, exciting, satisfying, and relatively harmless addiction, but it's an addiction all the same. Some cougars find it difficult not to overindulge, especially when the jungle is full of such tasty prey. Their personal slogan is "so many men, so little time."

This fact is clearly understood by younger partners. They are often very anxious about their cougar's ability to attract more like themselves. They may also be insecure about holding onto her in the face of such availability. Why should cougars resist shopping around? (Good question). Two words—time and stamina.

You may be loaded with money (having landed a huge settlement, a huge inheritance, or a well-deserved bonus), but few women feel they can or want to spend all day every day making love with vigorous young men. Oh, okay, not a good enough reason. All right. How about all the time that's taken up by being greedy? Since young men are constantly on the go, you could find you're stretched to your limit trying to juggle your time. They'll want you to join them when they play sports, party, go to movies, drive, bike, drink, dance, and eat out. It's all very exhausting.

You could give up your job and hire a live-in housekeeper in order to free up your time, but most cougars prefer to lead a more balanced life. They prefer to stick to one at a time and keep the others panting at the edge of the compound. After all, young men are like wine bottles—you can stack them up and they don't spoil.

Am I losing you here? Okay. How about considering health and safety? Monogamy is the best way to avoid disease. Serial monogamy is the next best thing.

Other Cougars

THIS MAY SEEM a strange inclusion to a neophyte cougar, but if you think about it, other older women could definitely pose a problem. Other cougars have sensitive whiskers. The fact that he's with you tells them that he loves older, not younger. The big grin on your face doesn't help either. Clearly he knows what they want and need.

If you ever want to see a real feeding frenzy, let your man loose in a room full of attractive older women. Whereas young women are blatant about stealing someone else's prey, older women can be really sneaky when it comes to getting his attention.

ANOTHER COUGAR WILL ...

- ☿ talk about her expensive new car, or the fact that she wants to buy a Ferrari—if only she could find someone to advise her
- ☿ discuss her next trip to an exclusive resort on Mustique, and mention that she's looking for someone to accompany her— just as an escort, of course
- ☿ mention that she knows Bill Gates and just can't seem to get around to accepting his invitation to visit

It's a jungle out there

- ask all about you (an excellent trick to discover what he finds so fascinating), and then say that she taught you everything you know
- pat his bum, put her hand on his knee, and listen avidly— even if he's talking about the price of beer
- say she owns shares in a brewery
- offer him a seat in a box at the next ball game—not mentioning that she'll be in the one next to it
- offer him money if he's really splendid (now that's sneaky)
- try the Sharon Stone *Basic Instinct* move when you're not looking (even sneakier)
- say that she's writing a book about older women and younger men and ask him to do lunch to discuss his experiences. (This works, by the way.)

Remember: it's a jungle out there, and the underbrush is thick with other prowling cougars. You may have to get an electric prod.

Money

TO SURVIVE IN the cougar world, you must have a basic understanding about money and younger men. You will probably have more than he does. You will probably be more successful than he is. Never mind the march of liberation, this still upsets a generally accepted social rule—the one that says man should have more of everything and take control of monetary matters.

For many younger men, a woman with her own means isn't a problem at all. They're as attracted to money and success as younger women are, and for all the same reasons. Well, mainly one—dating someone who has money and status translates into an easier life for them. They've also grown up in a world of equality and are comfortable sharing everything. The trouble arises when this share-and-share-alike attitude is applied to your money.

To be fair though, most younger men will offer to pay their way (unless he happens to be a gigolo-in-training). Some may even insists on being in charge financially, even if he can't afford it. This macho man routine can cause problems for the cougar used to living a certain lifestyle. While a more modest approach can be refreshing and even quite romantic now and then, the novelty soon wears off. Besides, it's upsetting to have someone faint when they hear what you paid for your Manolo Blahniks.

Over time, he might become resentful about what he sees as an imbalance in the relationship. Despite his comfort with women's liberation and equality, he can begin to feel emasculated by your monetary power. He might get tired of the bill always being handed to you (with a smirk by the waiter or salesperson), although he'll usually recover quite quickly— especially if you're buying him a Hugo Boss suit or an iMac.

For your part, you might get tired of paying for everything. You might develop a problem with his easy come, easy go attitude to money. You might get tired of your answering machine being filled up with messages from Visa and MasterCard. If this is the case, and you realize that you prefer the good old days when men controlled the money, you're hunting the wrong prey. Turn in your whiskers and become a canary.

Pets

PETS ARE THE Great Divide between all men and women, regardless of age. Men usually like dogs (the bigger the better) while women, especially cougars, love their cats. There's nothing like family when it comes down to it. Cougars are usually deeply attached to their cats. Experience has taught them that felines are more loving, considerate, faithful, and comforting than any husband or lover. Young men usually look with disdain upon animals that eat food from tiny tins marked Seafood in Tomato Sauce, or Chicken Chunks.

HIS DOG WILL ...

- growl every time you come near his master
- continually stuff its nose in your crotch
- bark to go outside at inopportune times, and then immediately want back in
- poop on your lawn
- chase your cat
- dig up your flowers
- slobber all over your furniture and clothes
- stand at the end of the bed, panting, while you're making love

YOUR CAT WILL ...

- sense that he hates cats and run over and sit on his lap
- sharpen its claws on his pants—when he's in them

- Y cry to be let out at inopportune times, and then immediately want back in
- Y throw up on his shoes when he's taken them off
- Y walk all over his new car with muddy paws
- Y tease his dog into a frenzy
- Y get hair all over his clothes and in his underwear
- Y climb onto the bed and perch on a moving body when you're making love

If you both have pets and decide to try a live-in relationship, they can be a deciding factor as to whether it lasts for more than two days. As a general rule, it doesn't make sense to date a man with a dog unless you adore dogs, too. If you try to come between a man and his beloved dog, know that you will lose. (Make sure that he knows the same about you and your cat.) If you do decide to give it the old college try, always plan ahead for allergy attacks (his and yours) by stocking up on antihistamines. Keeping a stack of lint rollers handy is not a bad idea either.

Prey Abuse

ANOTHER POTENTIAL relationship-breaker is a strong cougar's natural inclination to turn her adoring young man into a servant. I know—they're generally so handy around the house that it's very tempting to give him chores to do, especially if you want a break from the bedroom (really??). But it can backfire.

Even though you've assigned him a mundane task—such as unblocking the drains or cleaning your car—his mind will still be focused on things like sex, oral sex, and more sex. Once he's finished his task, he'll bounce into the house randy as a moose in heat. There goes your time again.

The problem is that some young men love the dominant mistress bit for a while, but may eventually tire of being taken for the handyman, even if the job does come with some pretty spectacular perks.

Disregard this hazard if the mistress/slave aspect turns both of you on.

Career Changes

WHEN I FIRST started dating younger men, I didn't consider career pressures at all. In the end, however, they became a major factor in the breakup of several relationships. Career changes—whether a relocation or just a shift in direction—can strongly affect cougars who have become attached to their prey.

Back in the old days, people got jobs and pursued their careers in one town or city. A move or change would occur only under the most dire of circumstances. These days, the job market is international. Young men who start out in one city may consider moving to further their ambitions, make more money, or simply find a job in their chosen field. When this happens, a cougar may be asked to consider packing up and moving along with him. Although some do, it's rare (unless he's wildly wealthy, of course).

Despite her partner's upwardly mobile status, she is probably well established in her own career. She probably likes where she lives and may have family responsibilities that prevent her from relocating. More importantly, she may not want to throw away her own life to start over again. Smart cougars will remember that the relationship will probably end prematurely. Giving up everything she has to follow a man into the unknown is contrary to everything that makes her a cougar.

Age is another factor. If the cougar is much older, she may already be viewing the future as a time for leisure and pleasure, a time for backing away from her previously all-consuming ambitions. Yet her younger man may just be reaching the peak of his career. For him, work may still be exciting, stimulating, and worthwhile. In other words, she may be thinking retirement. He will not.

Persuading a young man to give up everything to retire with you rarely happens. This may change if you're extremely wealthy and can offer him a Lifestyle of the Rich and Famous. If not, dust off your hunting gear and say bye-bye.

Snared!

IF YOUR AND YOUR young prey have some-how managed to survive all the traps and attacks described in the previous two chapters, you are in a Serious Relationship. Even if the "L-word" hasn't crossed your lips, it may have crossed his mind. It's a well-known fact that many young men will fall in love with the cougar that caught them. (Sounds like a James Bond movie.) If this does, in fact, happen, he will undoubtedly start talking about you with his family. If he's not talking, you can bet that they'll be pressing—they're dying to know what he's been up to and why he's so secretive about it. It's only a matter of time before your subjected to the test of all tests—meeting his mother.

I have only occasionally met the mothers of my younger dates, except when they became my younger husbands. It is a wise path for a cougar to take. The most difficult mothers I encountered were European. Some European women maintain a steadfast belief in the continuous and prolific provision of more children—despite the fact that their men carry on this noble tradition as much outside the marriage as in it. Even if they hailed from a country that admires and reveres its older women, they are still willing to burn cougars at the stake for diverting their young men from the procreative path.

Upon learning about my relationship with their sons, these women inevitably began a campaign of continuous son harass- ment—pleading, tears, and whining; not to mention late night phone calls demanding to know if their son was there. He was— right beside me in bed. And even if he was exhausted, satisfied, and totally relaxed, every fiber in his young body would spring to taut and anxious attention at the sound of her voice. As for getting him back in the mood? Forget it. Before the receiver was back in the cradle, he'd be pulling on his clothes for the return home. If he had his own place, the phone there would already be ringing when he arrived. Men with European backgrounds will inevitably capitulate to such pressure and move on to marriage and kids. A sensible cougar shrugs and moves onto the next younger man.

The Mother Mandate

GIVEN THE SHORT-TERM nature of most of their relationships, cougars rarely get to meet their preys' mothers. They don't want to. They don't want to bring their prey home to meet their own mother, either. Apart from the fact that she may be dead (or will be once she learns her daughter is dating someone young enough to be her grandson), it's not in the Cougar Mandate to meet parents.

The Mother Mandate is another thing. Mother will want to know all about you—who you are, what you do, and what you're doing with her son. She will give your poor man the third degree under the harsh glare of the kitchen lights. Unless he is unusually strong, withdrawn, or very mature for his age, he will tell all. Well, almost all. He will lie about your real age (if he knows), and about why he's dating an older woman. He will also be vague as to what you look like, and since there won't be any photos to show her (cougars don't encourage photos—they don't like to leave evidence behind) she'll be consumed with curiosity. If a meeting seems unavoidable, brace yourself. Fortifying with a couple of straight-up martinis helps.

As many an older cougar soon works out, problems arise when his mother is of a similar age. No matter how attractive, charming, and clever you are, you are certainly not what she had in mind as a partner for her son. (Disregard the above if you're rich or famous, on television or in the movies, or if you get your photo in the newspapers often—hopefully not for seducing young men.) Obviously, mothers prefer their sons to bring home nervous young girls with child-bearing hips. The mother is then in a position of superiority, a position of control. The world, especially the part that is connected to what lies beneath her son's pants, is revolving in the proper order and sequence.

However, if her darling boy does bring home an older woman, she will react with confusion and possibly anger. She will say that you have seduced her baby (probably using witchcraft). She will say that you have "stolen" him from her. She will view you as a rival. Her dreams of grandchildren will dissolve before her eyes. She will bemoan the fact that her son was supposed to carry on the family name, preferably with a nice girl of the same religion, color, or creed. Certainly of the same or similar age.

The only salve might be if she discovers you have plenty of money. "He always was a smart boy," she'll tell the rest of the family, secure in the knowledge that you'll dump him when you find out how much he spends. Even then, she will launch a sugar-sweet campaign to sabotage your relationship. She'll tell him to "have a good time while it lasts." She'll tell him to keep looking for "more suitable young women." She'll introduce him to the single daughters of every one of her friends.

All of this will fall on deaf ears. To the young man, you are most suitable indeed. You have introduced him to the wonderful world of cougars—a stimulating, educating, sophisticated, exciting, satisfying, stylish, and sexy world that he has wetly dreamed about since his voice deepened. Dating you means that he can enjoy it without the inconvenience of experience.

The Meeting Rules

THE MOTHER MEETING may be the one and only time that a cougar deviates from her normal behavior. Certain rules of decorum should be observed. If this seems painful and a little unfair, remember that it's only for a little while—and that the whole thing probably won't last past next week.

⅂ Dress appropriately. Although many cougars love their sexy clothes delightfully too tight and too short, this is not the time to wear them. Yes, I know that the word "appropriate" does not belong in a cougar's vocabulary, and I know all about the importance of Being Yourself, but you want to leave Mommy Dearest with the impression that you're doing her son a big favor, not that he's hired you for the evening. You are, after all, giving him an invaluable education in life. She should give you a medal.

⅂ Keep the visit short and sweet. The "hit and run" approach leaves little time for gross errors of judgment, foot-in-mouth episodes, or running makeup. Do what you have to do and get out.

⅂ Be empathetic. If she has a panic attack and calls for Prozac when you arrive, offer her one of yours.

⅂ Be thoughtful. Eat everything put in front of you even if you know it will cause hives. Praise her cooking but don't ask for the recipe. (You won't get it—her son might like yours better.)

⅂ Don't overindulge. Drinking too much will just encourage her to tell everyone that you're an alcoholic. Besides, a

Dress appropriately

smart cougar will have done her drinking before she arrived (try vodka—it doesn't smell). Smoke only if she does. If she doesn't, but her husband does, grit your teeth and bear it. Going outside to have a smoke with him will alienate her further—she'll think you're after him as well.

Y Be discreet. Don't mention sex, grab her son's butt, French-kiss him at the table, or tell her how "hot" he is. She secretly hopes that all you do is hold hands. Don't mention ex-husbands (no matter how many of them you've had), and steer the conversation away from kids—particularly if yours aren't far off her son's age.

Y Play it safe. Don't talk about religion, politics, or current world affairs—especially if their country of birth is embroiled in a war. Stick to the increase in traffic or the price of vegetables.

Y Stay ageless. If you are much older than him, don't date yourself by talking about the Vietnam War, the Beatles, or your Woodstock experience.

If his father takes you aside, be warm and friendly. He may offer you money to leave his son alone. Accept only if it's a large amount. If his mother welcomes you with open arms and tells you that you're the best thing that has ever happened to him, be wary. It may indicate that she's desperate to unload him.

Your Mother

MY BEST ADVICE? Don't do it. Say she recently passed away. You'll get sympathy and avoid further problems. If you do bring him home to meet your mother, it will be an automatic indicator of your real age (which you've hopefully lied about). Unless you are both genetic wonders who look twenty years younger than you are, he will be shocked that your mother is so *old*. Try telling him that you were a late baby, or that you were the first-ever post-menopausal in vitro implant embryo.

Don't let her show him pictures from when you were young, or from any of your weddings. Divert her from talking about previous boyfriends, especially if they were young too. When she asks what he does, jump in before he can say "unemployed" and offer "between careers." If she asks how old he is, add "isn't that wonderful!" when he replies. Kick her in the shins under the table if she mentions menopause.

On the side, expect her to tell you that he's just using you, that he's after your money, or that your father is upset. If she has a more positive attitude and is single herself, she may ask if his father is available. She'll tell you that it won't last. You'll happily agree.

Pouncing Back

THROUGHOUT THIS book, I've pointed out that cougars usually prefer short-term liaisons with their prey; but much of what I've written has focused on coping and enjoying a long-term, semi-permanent, or permanent relationship. This happens more often than people think. When it does, the cougar and her young man find that an age-gap partnership is not only solid, satisfying, interesting, and happy, but one that many people end up envying.

Why? It could be that such a pairing takes a lot more consideration and commitment than your run of the mill relationship. From the outset, both parties know that they're going against the flow of general conformity. This often creates a close-knit bond between the cougar and her partner. They lean on each other for strength, and have a vested interest in making things work so they can prove everyone wrong.

But as every woman knows, even the best laid plans can fall apart. In my own career as a cougar, a number of my relationships have turned into long-term affairs, including one that ended in marriage. Each ended as a result of some the factors I've covered here.

The marriage—to someone fourteen years my junior—was a truly great and interesting relationship that lasted for more than twelve years. It ended when my young husband felt he would find true fame, fortune, and recognition only in the Big Apple. We drifted apart on the long-distance relationship sea and eventually divorced. Unfortunately, the last I heard none of his dreams had come to pass.

A three-year relationship ended because his mother constantly harassed him about carrying on the family name. He bowed to her pressure and bought in to Procreation Panic. He sailed off into the sunset, married a young girl, had the necessary children, and then dumped her for another cougar.

One relationship that lasted for more than four years ended after he was downsized from his job. He relocated, convinced that his career would be renewed and rejuvenated in his new home. He asked me to go with him, but it was out of the question. I had a high media profile and very successful career. I owned my own home and had some considerable roots. Anyway, I had a book to write. But when the split came it still hurt like hell.

Most cougars will eventually face a breakup, and as with all other relationships (short or long, young or old) the split will be painful. The depth of her heartache will depend, in large part, on who did the dumping. It is often the cougar who decides to call it quits. She may look at her partner and realize that her love and/or lust for him has waned. She may be eager to hunt again. She may no longer feel comfortable with her current relationship. (What seems like a good idea at the outset can often pale over the course of time.) She may decide that she wants to explore other options.

One thing a true cougar will never do is succumb to outside pressures or feel insecure because of her age. If this does happen, and those fears turn into nagging paranoia, she'll drive her young prey back into the jungle. This is a clear sign that it's time she retired her cougar coat.

If the younger man ends the relationship, a cougar should be prepared to suffer for a while. Getting dumped always hurts. It doesn't matter if she knew it was coming or the relationship was lousy. It's still painful when it ends. Slinking away to lick her wounds helps, but pouncing back to her full, sleek, glory takes time, effort, and planning—plus copious amounts of alcohol and endless support and sympathy from friends. If anyone says "I told you so," a smart cougar will kick them in the shins.

Dump Do's and Don'ts

THE DAYS JUST after a relationship ends are dangerous indeed. Raw emotions float to the surface, and even the most experienced cougar may find herself entertaining some pretty uncharacteristic thoughts. Remember who and what you are, and keep the following "do's" and "don'ts" in mind.

DON'T ...

Y Drink and dial. I know it's very tempting to call him up when you've had one martini too many. You'll tell yourself that you're just going to say hi, or that you need to arrange a "pick up your stuff" meeting, but booze breaks down control. Before you know it, you'll be sobbing away, providing him with plenty of evidence to suggest that dumping you was the right thing to do. Very humiliating.

- Write angry/pleading/sexual/spiteful e-mails or letters. Apart from the fact someone else might read them, you'll regret most of what you said later. (Take it from someone who knows.)

- Go to "your" places. Steer clear of the place that you met, your favorite restaurant and bar, and the parkbench where you sat and smooched—at least for awhile. It will only make you mope even more and depress the people around you.

- Shut yourself away—especially from those you care about or who care about you. If you've been loudly whining for a long time, they could be avoiding you. You may have to repair some bridges.

- Neglect your appearance. It will only make you feel worse when you look in the mirror and will make others wonder what he saw in you.

- Sleep with his friends out of spite. (Well, only one of them if you must.) It won't make you feel any better—unless he's fabulous in bed.

Do ...

- ♈ Pamper yourself. Go to a spa or on vacation. If you can't get away, give yourself some TLC right at home.

- ♈ Get out of the house. Nothing says "I'm over you" more clearly than a cougar who's out on the town having some fun. The more people you meet, the better the chance to land new prey.

- ♈ Stay stylish. Get a new hairstyle, buy some sexy clothes or shoes, get even fitter and more toned. Consider cosmetic surgery if you think it will make you feel and look better and help you move confidently into the next stage of your life.

- ♈ Try something new. Immerse yourself in something that interests you, educates you, or furthers your career. Take up a new hobby. Try a new sport.

- ♈ Volunteer. Give it a try. It will make you feel better, even if you think you're the one in need of charity.

If you're thinking of giving up younger men, banish the thought from your mind. You should hunt again—the sooner, the better. There's no shortage of younger men, they're not

Happy hunting

illegal or fattening, and they're out there longing to be pounced on by someone as fabulous as you—so get going!

Above all, don't ever forget that you're a strong, sophisticated, independent, in control-of-your-life cougar. This breakup is a temporary glitch that will soon pass, leaving you free to start another adventure.

Happy hunting!

Acknowledgments

I'D LIKE TO thank my neighbor Valerie Peever for her invaluable computer help at home. Thanks also to the wonderful people at Key Porter Books—editor-in-chief Clare McKeon, whose vision made this book possible, inspired editor Linda Pruessen, publicity manager Lyn Cadence, and, of course, the awesome Anna Porter, president.